A detailed guide to every Major League city from the Northeast to the Southwest — and what to eat, see and do once you get there.

BASEBALL'S destinations

MLB
INSIDERS
CLUB

Baseball Insiders Library™

A detailed guide to every Major League city from the Northeast to the Southwest — and what to eat, see and do once you get there.

BASEBALL'S
destinations

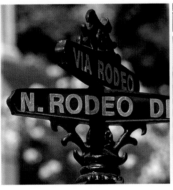

MLB
INSIDERS
CLUB

BASEBALL'S DESTINATIONS by Pete Williams

A detailed guide to every Major League city from the Northeast to the Southwest — and what to eat, see and do once you get there.

Printed in 2011

ABOUT THE AUTHOR

Pete Williams has covered Major League Baseball and Spring Training for nearly two decades for numerous media outlets, including USA Today, The New York Times, SportsBusiness Journal *and* Fox Sports. *The author or co-author of numerous books, including* Inside the World Series *and* Inside Spring Training *in the Baseball Insiders Library™, he lives with his wife and two sons in Safety Harbor, Fla.*

ACKNOWLEDGEMENTS

Major League Baseball would like to thank Pat Kelly and Milo Stewart Jr. at the National Baseball Hall of Fame and Museum for their invaluable assistance; as well as Eric Enders, Nathan Hale and Kristin Nieto for their diligent work in helping to prepare this book for publication.

MAJOR LEAGUE BASEBALL PROPERTIES

Vice President, Publishing
Donald S. Hintze

Editorial Director
Mike McCormick

Publications Art Director
Faith M. Rittenberg

Senior Production Manager
Claire Walsh

Associate Editor
Jon Schwartz

Associate Art Director
Melanie Finnern

Senior Publishing Coordinator
Anamika Panchoo

Project Assistant Editors
Chris Greenberg, Rachel Jacoby, Jodie Jordan

Editorial Intern
Daria Del Colliano, Harry Raymond

MAJOR LEAGUE BASEBALL PHOTOS

Director
Rich Pilling

Photo Editor
Jessica Foster

MLB INSIDERS CLUB

Creative Director
Tom Carpenter

Managing Editor
Jen Weaverling

Prepress
Wendy Holdman

2 3 4 5 6 7 8 9 10 / 12 11

ISBN: 978-1-58159-473-7

MLB Insiders Club
12301 Whitewater Drive
Minnetonka, MN 55343

TABLE OF CONTENTS

INTRODUCTION

With a large part of the Major League season played in the summer — when the kids are on vacation and the grownups wish they were — there's something about baseball that inspires wanderlust in fans across the country. For generations, baseball fans have attempted to see a game in every Big League ballpark. It's a goal that has become a moving target during the recent building boom. Like Ken Griffey Jr., who homered in more than 40 parks during his 22-year Hall of Fame career, a fan who began traveling in the early 1990s can now boast of watching games in far more buildings than the 30 active ones. And that means a whole new excuse to hit the road and explore each corner of the country — whether for the first time, or with a fresh set of eyes.

If you had just one day to capture the flavor of a community, there's a good chance that a trip to the ballpark would provide it in a microcosm. That's true not just in places like Boston and Chicago with historic baseball cathedrals, but also in the many communities that during the last two decades have built facilities combining classic baseball architecture with modern amenities and fan experiences. In places such as Baltimore, Denver and San Diego, baseball has even helped revitalize downtown areas, shifting the hearts of the cities.

For those intrepid hardball Magellans out there, these pages are a road map to excitement in all 26 Major League cities from coast to coast. Each of the six chapters represents one regional adventure that will take you from city to city and ballpark to ballpark. Trek from the South to the West Coast, by way of Texas, across the upper Midwest, down the Eastern Seaboard, and finally into the Heartland. This isn't just a baseball journey, but a trip around America.

No other sport is better woven into the fabric of a town. And that's what makes these Major League Baseball destinations so special — they all have a uniquely rich culture and energy, from the circadian rhythms of the working week to the nightlife districts, the skylines, cuisines, historical spots and local attractions. A city's baseball culture rarely ends at its Major League facility, which is why *Baseball's Destinations* also includes nearby Minor League teams and college programs, sports memorabilia shops and the sites of long-gone ballparks, as well as the sports bars and restaurants frequented by die-hard fans in any given town.

After a busy day of sightseeing, the lazy rhythms of the only major sport without a clock can be a welcome respite. Most fans already know that baseball is the destination. This book will show you how to enjoy the journey even more.

Boston's Yawkey Way is a bustling scene before a game at Fenway Park.

chapter 1

the south

ATLANTA

MIAMI

TAMPA

HOUSTON

ARLINGTON

Atlanta

Even before Hank Aaron, Eddie Mathews and the Braves departed Milwaukee and brought Major League Baseball to Atlanta for the 1966 season, there was a rich baseball tradition in the land of sweet tea and peach cobbler. Not only were many Big Leaguers Southern born — the prodigal Aaron prominent among them — but also the Atlanta Crackers were a powerhouse in the Southern Association.

HOME OF THE BRAVES

For more than 50 years prior to the debut of the Braves in Atlanta, the only thing "Minor League" about the capital of Georgia was its ballclub — and it was still pretty darn good. The Minor League club in Atlanta, oddly dubbed the Crackers, won more games than any other Southern Association club from 1901 through 1961 and featured budding Hall of Famers Luke Appling and Mathews — the only player to suit up for the Braves in Boston, Milwaukee and Atlanta. Beloved Detroit Tigers broadcaster Ernie Harwell also launched his Hall of Fame career with the Crackers before the club traded his contract to the Brooklyn Dodgers for catcher Cliff Dapper — likely the only time a player has ever been swapped for a broadcaster.

Although the Braves never had a losing season during their 13 years in Milwaukee, Chicago businessman Bill Bartholomay had dreams of bringing Major League Baseball to the South and began looking for a larger market below the Mason-Dixon line after he bought the team in 1962. Atlanta obliged on both fronts, and the Braves moved for the 1966 season.

Less than a decade into their stay, Atlanta-Fulton County Stadium was the stage for one of the most memorable moments in Big League history. After an arduous chase, Hank Aaron cracked his 715th career home run — one more than Babe Ruth had hit during his record-setting playing days — during the home opener in 1974.

"I don't know where Hank Aaron will break [Babe] Ruth's record," Mathews mused in the prelude to that fateful blow. "But I can tell you one thing: 10 years from the day he hits it, 3 million people will say they were there."

And true to Mathews' words, half of Atlanta would later claim to have been in the crowd that evening when Aaron took Los Angeles Dodgers pitcher Al Downing deep over the left-field wall in the fourth inning.

With media magnate Ted Turner providing the large broadcast platform for the club that Bartholomay was looking for, both the Braves and Turner's television empire — featuring WTBS and CNN — benefited greatly from the team's move to Georgia. Eccentric and hard-charging, Turner purchased the club outright in 1976 and developed a national following for "America's Team" in the early days of cable television.

Despite the play of 1980s stars Dale Murphy and Phil Niekro, enduring success proved elusive. That changed when a talented pitching staff featuring Steve Avery, Tom Glavine, Greg Maddux and John Smoltz lifted the club to dominance. With six NL Cy Young Awards between them during their time with the club, the trio backed up a lineup starring switch-hitting All-Star Chipper Jones.

In 1991, the Braves went from worst to first in the NL West and reached

Hank Aaron (left, scoring) is greeted by teammates after his record-setting 715th career home run. The "Tomahawk Chop" caught on with Braves fans during the team's dominant run in the 1990s.

11

the World Series, the first of 14 straight postseasons under skipper Bobby Cox. Featuring standouts like David Justice, Fred McGriff, Andruw Jones and Javy Lopez, the Braves were the most successful team of the '90s — their crowning achievement coming with a triumph over the Cleveland Indians in the 1995 World Series.

SOUTHERN FRIED FANDOM

From Eddie Mathews to Dale Murphy, the Atlanta Braves are best known for their stoic, classy, down-to-earth icons. Braves fans seem to take their cue from the club's low-key stars. They're passionate and loyal, but rarely mean-spirited or aggressive. In part due to this mild-mannered cheering style, Braves fans sometimes get knocked for being only mildly interested. Those rooting for less successful teams during the 1990s even complained that the fans were spoiled by success. But hearing one cacophonous "Tomahawk Chop" would surely prove doubters wrong.

"The Chop" was adapted from a tradition at Florida State University and arrived in Atlanta when FSU-standout Deion Sanders was playing for the home team. For the better part of a decade, the most dominant college football program and National League ballclub had the entire South chanting in unison.

Until Major League Baseball arrived in Florida in the 1990s with the birth of the Rays and Marlins, the Braves had the entire region to themselves. Of course, the franchise also had a national following thanks to its games being televised coast to coast on WTBS.

But even with fans across the country pulling for the team, and the long run of success from 1991–2005, all professional sports teams in Atlanta face stiff competition for the attention of local fans. The biggest sports acronyms in Atlanta are not MLB, NFL, NBA or NHL, but SEC and UGA. The Southeastern Conference and University of Georgia athletics are huge throughout the state and the rest of the South, especially on Saturdays in the fall when the Georgia Bulldogs football team takes to the gridiron against one of their regional rivals like Florida or Auburn.

THE PEACHTREE CIRCUIT

Although Turner Field is the hub of baseball in Atlanta, it's not the only place to see top-notch play. Georgia Tech, located in midtown Atlanta, has one of the nation's best college baseball programs and has produced Big League standouts such as Mark Teixeira, Matt Wieters, Jason Varitek and Nomar Garciaparra.

Another stop on the local hardball circuit is in nearby Gwinnett County, where the Braves' Triple-A team, the Gwinnett Braves, relocated in 2009 after playing for many years in Richmond, Va.

For those willing to travel a bit farther afield, the Ty Cobb Museum is 90 miles northeast of Atlanta in Royston, Ga., and well worth the trip for fans of "The Georgia Peach."

Anyone looking for a keepsake from their diamond tour of the Peach Tree State should stop by B.P. Sports Collectibles in the suburb of Marietta. The store has a huge inventory of Braves goods, as well as memorabilia from other teams. The shop has hosted dozens of high-profile autograph signings, and could provide a chance to meet a past or present Braves player.

If sightseeing works up your appetite, then consider Ted's Montana Grill the place to eat. The Western-themed

bison chain, founded by Ted Turner, has multiple locations in the Atlanta area to grab some good grub.

HOT 'LANTA

When Hank Aaron broke Babe Ruth's career home run mark during the home opener in 1974, it was the culmination of a long journey for the Alabama-born slugger. Aaron's stoic demeanor in the face of those who hoped for his failure, made him a role model during a turbulent time in American history. But no Atlanta figure did more to promote equality for all than Martin Luther King Jr. No trip is complete without a visit to his home in the Sweet Auburn area.

Grant Park is home to the Atlanta Cyclorama and Civil War Museum. The Atlanta Cyclorama is an expansive cylindrical panoramic painting — once the largest oil painting in the world — depicting the Battle of Atlanta.

Also in Grant Park, Zoo Atlanta is a 40-acre wildlife park that opened in 1889. Atlanta's oldest cultural attraction, it features more than 1,000 animals, including the endangered giant panda. It's less than a mile from Turner Field.

The Braves celebrate their 1995 World Series title (left). Atlanta-based Coca-Cola is a staple at Turner Field.

The Buckhead neighborhood in the northern part of town is referred to as the "Beverly Hills of the South" because of its concentration of wealth and upscale shopping. It's also a popular restaurant and nightlife destination.

The World of Coca-Cola, which opened to the public in 2007 after relocating and replacing the original exhibit, features the history of the iconic Atlanta-based beverage company. It's twice the size of the original attraction near Underground Atlanta and offers visitors a chance to enjoy a tour, listen to popular jingles from over the years, view hundreds of artifacts, and sample 60 Coke products from around the world.

The Georgia Aquarium, billed as the largest in the world — with more than 8 million gallons of water attractions — sits adjacent to the World of Coca-Cola. Other downtown attractions include CNN Center, where it's possible to take a 55-minute guided studio tour of the cable news operation; the High Museum of Art, with 11,000 pieces from the 19th and 20th centuries; and the Georgia Tech campus. Centennial Olympic Park, near CNN Center, is a popular gathering spot and hosts events throughout the year.

Popular suburban destinations for visitors include Six Flags over Georgia and Stone Mountain Park.

WHAT'S IN A NAME?

Under the ownership of political bigwig James Gaffney in 1912, the National League's Boston Doves (named after previous owners, the Dovey Brothers) sought to find a new name. Gaffney had ties to New York City political machine Tammany Hall (named after a Lenni-Lenape Indian Chief) whose members were known as Braves. From then on the franchise kept the moniker — even after moves to Milwaukee and Atlanta.

A balmy summer night at Turner Field (left) and a guided tour of the downtown CNN Center top off a trip to Atlanta.

Miami

With its sun-splashed beaches, verdant palm trees, myriad fishing spots, and year-round warm weather, South Florida has long been a popular haven for Major League Baseball teams from less hospitable locales during the cold winter months. Proximity to Central America, Cuba and the Caribbean has also ensured that the "Gateway to the Americas" is a hotbed for up-and-coming talent.

FISH STORIES

Perhaps it's the annual presence of Spring Training or the unique influence of the Latin culture from nearby Cuba, but Miami has never wanted for baseball. The city welcomed the Boston Braves for Spring Training as early as 1916, and hosted the Brooklyn Dodgers, New York Giants, Philadelphia Phillies and Pittsburgh Pirates before 1950. The Baltimore Orioles trained in Miami from 1959–90, and returned to South Florida in 1996.

The Miami Marlins played in the International League from 1956–60, and the Marlins name was resurrected in 1962 for a Florida State League team, now the Fort Myers Miracle. Despite such credentials, it was an upset when Wayne Huizenga, a South Florida entrepreneur and owner of the NFL's Dolphins, landed an MLB expansion franchise in 1990, getting the nod over Tampa Bay and its already-built Florida Suncoast Dome.

The latest iteration of the Marlins made its Big League debut on April 5, 1993, defeating the Dodgers behind a 4-for-4 performance by Jeff Conine. Conine would go on to earn the nickname "Mr. Marlin" and be the only member of both the 1997 and 2003 World Series-winning teams. Game 7 of the '97 Series was an extra-inning classic in which the Marlins came from behind to capture South Florida's first professional sports championship before 67,204 rapt fans at Pro Player Stadium.

"Around the seventh inning I started to think it was going to be a classic, maybe go to extra innings," Florida pitching coach Larry Rothschild told *Sports Illustrated*. "The tension was there with every pitch."

Both the '97 and '03 clubs were surprise contenders that earned playoff berths. In both instances, after the World Series rings were handed out, ownership aggressively reconfigured the roster to stay young and fiscally responsible. After winning the 2003 crown, the Marlins added fresh talent, like shortstop Hanley Ramirez, and they are now looking forward to their new ballpark in the Little Havana neighborhood.

BIG FANS

With games played in stifling summer heat and amidst the cloudbursts that characterize much of the baseball season in South Florida, the Marlins have sometimes struggled to draw large crowds. But make no mistake about it, this team has a *large* following.

In 2008, the club introduced the "Marlins Manatees," an all-male dance troupe composed of heavy-set supporters who were eager to strut their stuff for fellow fans at the ballpark in order to help energize the crowd during Marlins home games.

FISHING HOLE

Dolphins founder Joe Robbie had baseball in mind when he designed the multi-purpose stadium that bore his name when it opened in 1987. The outfield fence at the park — now known as Sun Life Stadium — has various signature quirks and crannies. Sight lines are good for baseball with the exception of certain seats sold only during the postseason that have an obstructed view of part of the outfield.

Billy the Marlin (above) and baseball fans throughout South Florida have cheered on the Marlins during successful trips to the Fall Classic in 1997 and 2003. Craig Counsell scored the dramatic Series-winning run in the 11th frame of Game 7 in 1997 (right).

The massive video scoreboards and sound system, created for 70,000 football fans, provides a multimedia experience many newer baseball stadiums can't rival. Plus, Billy the Marlin appears regularly throughout the park.

Despite the myriad recreational opportunities in South Florida — from beaches to boutiques — fans coming to the park can still enjoy an authentic South Florida experience thanks to palm trees, the teal-and-orange color scheme and ever-present Latin music. Best of all, there's plenty of local cuisine throughout the building, including Cuban sandwiches, conch fritters and black beans and rice.

START YOUR ENGINES

Visiting gearheads should speed over to Homestead-Miami International Speedway, home of NASCAR's season finale, as well as the season-ending races for IndyCar and three other racing series. The track's architecture and color scheme reflect the art deco design of nearby Miami Beach.

The University of Miami's baseball team is a national powerhouse and plays its games on the school's picturesque campus in Coral Gables. The program has sent dozens of players to the Majors, including Ryan Braun, Aubrey Huff, Greg Vaughn, Pat Burrell, Charles Johnson and Alex Fernandez.

BEACH BUMS AND MILLIONAIRES

There's no shortage of things to do in and around Miami, although many visitors flock to South Beach for its nightlife, restaurants and Art Deco hotels, others prefer nearby Fort Lauderdale, which has transformed from a spring break location into a quieter, more upscale version of South Beach. From the

WHAT'S IN A NAME?

The marlin is a game fish long revered by fishermen in South Florida for being a tough catch. But in addition to the tenacious species, Florida can attribute its moniker to the Minor Leagues. From the 1950s through the '80s, various Miami-based clubs hooked the name Marlins; soon, the Major Leagues followed suit.

shopping and restaurants of Las Olas Boulevard to the Venice-like waterways that run through some neighborhoods to the ever-famous beach, Fort Lauderdale remains a popular tourist destination. Seamheads should note that it's just as convenient to get to Land Shark Stadium as Miami, although it will be further from the new ballpark.

South Florida boasts some world famous beaches, with pristine coastline stretching from Palm Beach to Key West. At the northern end of Miami Beach is the exclusive Bal Harbour, home to luxury resorts and the Bal Harbour Shops, which feature designers like Versace, Louis Vuitton and Prada, among others. One can also check out cruise ships docked in Miami's waters and see the Miami Children's Museum, a cool place for kids to enjoy interactive exhibits.

For many visitors, no trip to South Florida is complete without an airboat tour of the Florida Everglades, one of the world's largest wetland areas. There it's possible to glimpse alligators and other species in their natural habitats. For those who prefer to see wildlife in a more controlled environment, the Zoo Miami is one of the nation's best, with more than 80 exhibits and 1,300 animals.

PLANES, TRAINS & AUTOMOBILES

Sun Life Stadium, although located in North Miami, is more convenient to Fort Lauderdale-Hollywood International Airport, which many travelers prefer over the far busier Miami International. Driving in South Florida can be an adventure, but cars are a must because of limited public transportation as well the distance from the ballpark to beaches, hotels and other attractions.

With its famed Art Deco hotels along Collins Avenue, Miami Beach is one of the most picturesque areas of the country.

Tampa Bay

Although folks in the rest of the country may not have taken Tampa baseball seriously until the baby-faced Rays knocked off the veteran Red Sox to win the AL pennant in 2008, fans in the area may be as well versed in the game as anyone in the country. St. Petersburg Mayor Al Lang drew the Philadelphia Phillies to town in 1915, and created a bond with the game that has thrived in the region for nearly a century.

HOPE SPRINGS ETERNAL

The Tampa Bay region — which includes the communities of Tampa, St. Petersburg and Clearwater — was the spring home for the New York Yankees for 34 years. Similarly, the Cardinals spent 51 years at Al Lang Field, sharing it intermittently with the New York Mets and Baltimore Orioles. Across the bay in Tampa, Al Lopez Field — named after the Hall of Fame catcher and manager — hosted the Cincinnati Reds for more than three decades. In 1996, the Yankees moved their spring home from Fort Lauderdale to Tampa's Legends Field, since renamed in honor of longtime team owner and local resident George Steinbrenner.

Despite being a preeminent Spring Training destination, landing a year-round MLB franchise proved difficult for Tampa Bay. In 1986, the city of St. Petersburg built the Florida Suncoast Dome in the hopes of luring the White Sox from Chicago, but that plan never came to fruition, and it would be 12 years before the building hosted its own Major League club. In the interim, the city flirted with the San Francisco Giants and hosted other sporting events, including full NHL and Arena Football seasons. St. Petersburg finally got its wish for a permanent Big League club, and on March 31, 1998, Hall of Famers Ted Williams, Stan Musial, Monte Irvin and Al Lopez threw out ceremonial first pitches before Tampa Bay's first regular-season game. The Devil Rays lost to the Tigers, 11-6, and would struggle in their infancy due to the rigors of starting a club from scratch. In 2005, 28-year-old Andrew Friedman took over the role of general manager and built a talented team through the draft. The club dropped "Devil" from its name for the 2008 season, changed its color scheme from green to blue, and rode the talents of homegrown players like Evan Longoria and B.J. Upton, all the way to the 2008 World Series.

DEVIL'S ADVOCATES

When it comes to baseball, Tampa Bay is a place of contradictions. In fact, it's not even a single city, but a body of water and a catch-all civic moniker created for the NFL's expansion Buccaneers (who are housed at Raymond James Stadium, the former site of Al Lopez Field) in 1976 to refer to the communities of Tampa, St. Petersburg and Clearwater as a united front.

Tampa Bay has a longer history with Spring Training than any other locale in the country. But that hasn't always translated into support for the local Rays. Many northern transplants remain loyal to their hometown teams, while many older natives support longtime spring residents such as the Phillies, Yankees, Blue Jays, Reds or Cardinals. The Yanks, Jays, Cards and Phils also field Minor League teams in the Class-A Florida State League. Other fans feel compelled

PLANES, TRAINS & AUTOMOBILES

Tampa International Airport has consistently been rated among the nation's best — including earning top marks from *Condé Nast Traveler* — and services most of the country via non-stop flights. Since the Rays play in St. Petersburg and the communities of Tampa, St. Petersburg and Clearwater are separated by water and connected by bridges, this is a rental car town. Public transportation is minimal, and you won't see many taxis.

Third baseman Evan Longoria (left) helped guide the Rays to the 2008 World Series, delighting fans at Tropicana Field.

to root for the myriad locals that populate rosters around the Majors.

Although Tampa Bay is the nation's 19th largest market, it has produced perhaps more players per capita than any other community. The list of hometown stars includes Hall of Famers Al Lopez and Wade Boggs, along with Steve Garvey, Lou Piniella, Gary Sheffield, Dwight Gooden, Fred McGriff, Tino Martinez, Luis Gonzalez, Howard Johnson, Brad Radke and Marlins outfielder Chris Coghlan, the 2009 NL Rookie of the Year.

"There's a lot of dedication from the Little League age on up," says Tampa area native and former Big League first and third baseman Dave Magadan. "Spring Training is down there with a lot of teams. I think that makes baseball a natural draw for a young kid."

For years, Tampa Bay sports fans followed football first, especially with the turn-of-the-century success of the Buccaneers and the more recent dominance of the University of Florida Gators. That has changed, though, with the Rays' success. These days, fans in the region are increasingly likely to be sporting a tee shirt emblazoned with "Crawford" or "Longoria" instead of a football jersey.

THE TROPICANA EXPERIENCE

"The Trop" is the last of baseball's non-retractable domed stadiums. After MLB placed an expansion franchise in the Tampa Bay area in 1995, the building known as the Thunderdome — the name given to the cacophonous venue when the NHL's Tampa Bay Lightning were drawing record crowds in the early '90s — was re-christened Tropicana Field and underwent a $70 million upgrade. By the time the Trop finally hosted the Devil Rays' first Big League game in 1998, baseball was in the midst of a retro-ballpark boom. To keep up with newer parks, team officials installed such fan-friendly attractions as a "touch tank" with live cow-nosed Rays just beyond the fence in right-center field, the Ted Williams Museum and a host of interactive, kid-friendly games. The Batter's Eye Restaurant beyond center field offers a great view of the action and the Cuesta-Rey Cigar Bar is the only one of its kind in any MLB ballpark. The Rays play in climate-controlled 72 degrees and were the first professional sports team to install FieldTurf, a softer substitute for AstroTurf.

Despite the recent add-ons, visitors still have at least one complaint about the Trop — actually four complaints. Four catwalks hang down from the roof and occasionally interfere with play.

The catwalks are lettered A through D. Any ball touching the A Ring, or the in-play portion of the B Ring, can drop for a hit or be caught for an out. The C and D Rings are out of play; if they are struck between the foul poles, then the ball is ruled a home run. It can be hard enough to track a ball popped high into the air without trying to remember the various rules for each of the catwalks. Or what to do if the ball doesn't come down at all, which has been known to happen on occasion.

SIGHTS BY THE BAY

The weather and outdoor recreational opportunities are the prime attractions of the Tampa Bay area. Two of the region's beaches — Fort DeSoto Park in St. Petersburg and Caladesi Island near Dunedin — have each been rated America's No.1 Beach by Stephen Leatherman, a.k.a. "Dr. Beach," who ranks America's top shore spots.

To complete the geographic triad, Clearwater Beach is a popular destination for college spring breakers, but is relatively quiet the rest of the year. The city has built a waterfront pedestrian walkway recently, but even with development on the strip, Clearwater retains its kitschy old-Florida feel.

For a day away from the beach, Busch Gardens theme park is a must-do for thrill seekers, while Lowry Park Zoo — rated the nation's No.1 zoo for kids by *Parents* magazine in 2009 — counts creatures from Africa and Australia as its residents. Alternatively, the Florida Aquarium is one of Tampa Bay's underrated attractions, with dozens of sea critters and a spray park. Kids will also enjoy the Museum of Science and Industry, an interactive attraction not far from Busch Gardens.

The Salvador Dali Museum in St. Petersburg celebrates the life and work of the Spanish surrealist. For a real ecological trip, visit Sunken Gardens, just north of downtown St. Pete. It's a six-acre botanical garden featuring more than 500 species of plants.

Head north to Tarpon Springs, which has the largest Greek community outside of Greece and is *the* place to go for gyros, souvlaki and baklava.

WHAT'S IN A NAME?

Major League Baseball came to Tampa Bay in 1995, and locals deluged the organization with prospective names, culminating in a choice between the Manta Rays or the Devil Rays. Originally dubbed the Tampa Bay Devil Rays, the club decided to start anew in 2008. It dropped the "Devil," but stuck with the Rays moniker, as it offered continuity and pointed toward a bright future.

Clearwater Beach (opposite) is one of many beaches in the Tampa Bay area. Wade Boggs (above) collects his 3,000th career hit with the then-Devil Rays in 1999.

Houston

Contrary to popular belief, baseball in Houston didn't begin when the Astrodome landed from outer space in 1965. The largest city in the Lone Star State was home to the Minor League Houston Buffaloes from as far back as 1907, when they played in the Texas League. When the beloved "Buffs" joined the American Association in 1959, native Texan Dan Rather handled play-by-play duties on the radio.

HOUSTON, WE HAVE A BIG LEAGUE CLUB

A longtime Cardinals affiliate, the Houston Buffaloes featured Dizzy Dean and Joe Medwick and bounced around various Minor League circuits until the Big Leagues expanded to Texas in the 1960s. From 1939–41, the Buffs won three straight Texas League titles, averaging 100 wins a season. In 1959, the club moved to the American Association.

With Houston officials frustrated in their attempts to land a Major League team, the city became one of eight sites for a proposed "Continental League," which would contend with the already-established American and National Leagues. Rather than face competition from an upstart circuit, Major League Baseball awarded New York and Houston NL franchises for the 1962 season. The Houston team began as the Colt .45s and played home games at Colt Stadium, known for its high temperatures and high concentration of rattlesnakes. Three years later, the team moved into the space age Astrodome and was rebranded the Astros in deference to the local aerospace industry.

Neither the name change nor the building improved the fortunes of the team, which did not win a division title until 1980. That Astros club, led by pitchers Joe Niekro and Texas native Nolan Ryan, and outfielders Cesar Cedeno and Jose Cruz, would set the tone for a competitive decade to come. Ryan left after the '88 season and the team slumped in the early 1990s, only to re-emerge behind the "Killer B's," Jeff Bagwell and Craig Biggio. The Astros reached the playoffs four times from 1997–2001 and won the franchise's first National League pennant in 2005, led by Manager Phil Garner and pitchers Roy Oswalt, Andy Pettitte and Roger Clemens, the last two being Texas residents.

DOWN TO EARTH

There are many reasons that All-Stars Jeff Bagwell and Craig Biggio spent their entire Big League careers — 35 seasons combined — in Houston, one being the friendly, warm relationship between the ballclub and Astros fans.

"I couldn't have scripted it any better," Biggio said after notching the 3,000th hit of his career at Minute Maid Park on June 28, 2007. "I worked hard here and they appreciated that. As a baseball player, the way the fans treated me... I've said for a long time — I love these guys, I love this city."

Despite being the fourth-largest city in the nation, Houston is still a close-knit community. That atmosphere carries over to the baseball club that has quietly been one of the game's more consistent over the last three decades, posting just one last-place finish from 1976 through 2009.

Players enjoy the under-the-radar atmosphere of Houston and the warm reception they receive from fans throughout the Gulf Coast region.

Just as knowledgeable but not as demanding as other fanbases, local supporters have always embraced the sometimes-quirky organization, never seeming to mind the indoor, artificial-turf environment of the Astrodome or even the sartorially suspect "Tide Box" uniforms of the 1970s. A stoic group, throughout the years Astros fans have rallied around offbeat players such as

Minute Maid Park (above) provides a modern gameday experience for Astros fans, featuring a train (right) that moves along a track on top of the exterior wall beyond left field whenever an Astros player hits a home run or the team wins a game.

Larry Dierker, Joe Niekro, Larry Andersen and Jose Lima, and suffered through the unfortunate trade of Joe Morgan and Cesar Geronimo to the Reds, and J.R. Richard's incredibly tragic stroke.

MAID IN TEXAS
Given the team's eclectic stadium history, perhaps it's appropriate that Minute Maid Park includes such unique features as Tal's Hill, the 30-degree center-field slope (complete with a flagpole) in the spirit of "The Terrace" at Cincinnati's bygone Crosley Field, and a 1860s-replicated locomotive on tracks above left field that heralds big moments during the game.

"Squeeze Play" is an interactive entertainment center designed for fans 12 and under. Youngsters can test their pitch speed or hitting prowess and, of course, indulge in a slushy at the Minute Maid juice bar. Junction Jack, the Astros'

jackrabbit mascot, also makes appearances at every home game.

Minute Maid Park has some of baseball's best food and drink options. The signature food item is a loaded baked potato — a massive spud

PLANES, TRAINS & AUTOMOBILES
It's a 30-35 minute cab ride from George Bush Intercontinental Airport to downtown Houston, but once you're in the downtown or Galleria areas, you won't have to travel far to find anything you want. If you opt to rent a car, that's no problem, as there are more than 25,000 parking spaces within walking distance of Minute Maid Park. If you're looking for mass transit, Houston's METRO provides public transportation in the form of buses, light rail and vans, but doesn't have any connections to the nearby suburbs.

smothered in pulled pork, barbecue sauce, onions and jalapeno peppers. Fans can wash down such rib-sticking meals with a drink at Larry's Big Bamboo, named for longtime Houston pitcher and broadcaster Larry Dierker's favorite Spring Training hangout in Kissimmee, Fla. Larry's spot also features chicken wings, burgers and fish tacos. The FiveSeven Grille restaurant in center field is named in tribute to No. 5, Jeff Bagwell, and No. 7, Craig Biggio, offering Texas-sized portions of steaks, desserts and cocktails.

MORE HOUSTON BASEBALL ...

The Nolan Ryan Foundation and Exhibit Center is located in nearby Alvin, Texas, and is part of Alvin Community College. The Exhibit Center opened in 1999, and includes displays, videos and memorabilia from the Hall of Famer's illustrious career.

Houston-based TriStar Productions stages some of the largest baseball memorabilia shows in the country, many at Houston's own George R. Brown Convention Center. TriStar, an official MLB licensee, hosts many private autograph signings and markets trading cards of recent MLB draft picks.

After emerging as a three-sport star at Houston's Jefferson Davis High, Carl Crawford was a second-round selection of the Tampa Bay Rays in 1999. With Texas residents like Andy Pettitte and Roger Clemens returning to the Lone Star State to pitch for the Astros later in their careers, Houston baseball fans can still dream that Crawford will come home some day.

Despite the team's move to Minute Maid Park in 2000, the Astrodome still stands in Reliant Park, though it has hosted few major events in recent years.

SPACE CITY

When the local baseball club is known as the Astros, it's a good bet that there is a prominent aerospace presence in town. And Space Center Houston does not disappoint. It's the only place in the world where visitors can see astronauts train for missions, touch a real moon rock, land a (simulated) shuttle and take a behind-the-scenes tour of NASA.

When the Astrodome opened in 1965, the groundscrew fittingly dressed in space suits (left). Houston's Big League entrant was dubbed the Colt .45s (above) when it debuted in 1962, but later became the Astros to pay tribute to the local aerospace industry (top).

When Houston was awarded an expansion franchise for the 1962 season, a naming contest was held and "Colt .45s" won out. When the club moved to the Astrodome in 1964 it took on its namesake, becoming the Astros. The name developed from Houston's role in the aerospace industry. The club moved to its current park in 2000 and decided to hold on to the space age moniker.

For those with terrestrial interests, there's plenty to do in downtown Houston, home to three major sports venues and popular theater districts. Main Street, just blocks from Minute Maid Park, has dance clubs, pubs and upscale restaurants. Those looking for a diversion from baseball will find opera, ballet, the symphony and the Theater District within walking distance, too.

The Houston Zoo features 4,500 animals and represents more than 800 species. There are also plenty of museums, including the interactive Children's Museum of Houston, the Houston Museum of Natural Science and the Museum of Fine Arts.

Although "Space City" is home to world-class museums, food is perhaps the city's biggest attraction. Houston is known for some of the country's best barbecue, especially at the three locations of Goode Company. All sorts of grub can be found in the Galleria area, which also includes one of the country's largest shopping malls. Water Wall is a city landmark located near the Galleria, dropping thousands of gallons of water 64 feet every minute.

Another staple of Texas culture is the rodeo. For those heading to town in March, the famous Houston Livestock Show and Rodeo, also known as Rodeo Houston, is the world's largest livestock exhibition and most prestigious event on the professional rodeo circuit.

Astros fans eagerly cheered on Craig Biggio as the lifelong Houston player worked his way toward 3,000 career hits.

Arlington

Young baseball fans deep in the heart of Texas could be forgiven for thinking that hard-throwing Alvin, Texas native Nolan Ryan introduced the national pastime to his home state and forged the Texas Rangers franchise with his bare hands. But the truth is that the neighboring cities of Dallas and Forth Worth fielded clubs in the Texas League, dating all the way back to the 1800s and that Texas has a storied baseball past.

NOT-SO-LONE RANGERS

For nine innings on Aug. 22, 1989, Nolan Ryan looked more like the flamethrower that broke into the Major Leagues with the New York Mets in 1966 than a 42-year-old vet just a few years from retirement. In front of more than 40,000 fans at Arlington Stadium, Ryan struck out 13 Oakland Athletics batters, including future Hall of Famer Rickey Henderson. For a player who would finish his career with a record seven no-hitters, a 13-strikeout game wasn't something to get too excited about. But neither Ryan nor any of the fans in attendance would forget this one: When Henderson swung and missed at the third strike to lead off the top of the fifth inning, he became the 5,000th Major Leaguer to ride the "Ryan Express" back to his seat in the dugout.

"'It was an honor to be the 5,000th," Henderson quipped after the game. "As Davey Lopes says, 'If he ain't struck you out, you ain't nobody.'"

In Ryan's five years with the team before his retirement in 1993, the club never reached the postseason. All together, it took the franchise more than two decades from its 1972 move to the Lone Star State from Washington to play meaningful October baseball. The team turned a corner after Rangers Ballpark at Arlington opened its doors in 1994. The club won the AL West crown three times in the late '90s thanks to stars like Ivan "Pudge" Rodriguez, Juan Gonzalez and Rafael Palmeiro. During the following decade, the Rangers assembled big-slugging teams tailored to suit the demeanor of the fans and the hitter-friendly ballpark, notably landing free agent superstar shortstop Alex Rodriguez in 2001. Rodriguez put up historic numbers in Arlington and nabbed his first Most Valuable Player Award during the three seasons he played in a Rangers uniform. In 2008, Ryan became the team's president and re-vamped the strategy around pitching and defense, with an emphasis on the speed of Elvis Andrus, Julio Borbon and Ian Kinsler.

Although success was a longtime coming, Dallas first had a pro baseball club in 1888. The franchise operated as the Griffins, Giants, Marines, Submarines, Steers, Rebels and Eagles before becoming the Rangers in their last Texas League season in 1958. The club in nearby Fort Worth was known as the Panthers from 1902–31, before becoming the Cats. In 1959, the American Association expanded and added both cities. Dallas outdrew Fort Worth but the teams merged and became the top farm club of the Kansas City Athletics in 1960. The Dallas-Fort Worth Rangers were then affiliated with the Angels for the next two seasons, before joining the Pacific Coast League in 1963 as a Twins affiliate. In 1964, the team competed as the Dallas Rangers, affiliated again with the Athletics before moving to Vancouver. With the Minor League club's departure, the Texas League created the Dallas-Fort Worth Spurs to play in the new Turnpike Stadium for 1965. The team lasted through 1971 before giving way to the region's first Major League squad.

TAKE ME OUT TO THE BALLPARK

Even if Rangers Ballpark is located in a suburban area of Dallas, the club's home field since 1994 replicates the downtown vibe and aesthetic nature that made Camden Yards such a hit when it debuted in Baltimore in 1992. The stadium features exposed steel, red brick and asymmetrical outfield dimensions. For all its urban touches, though, the park is still Texas-sized, with a mammoth three-deck grandstand and a four-story office complex that connect to enclose the ballpark. The enclosed nature is unique compared to many other stadiums that are con-structed to leave an open view of the skyline.

With a lack of foul territory, Rangers Ballpark provides an intimate viewing experi-ence, especially for fans sitting on the field level. There's also plenty to eat, particu-larly Tex-Mex, barbecue and the park's signature dish — smoked turkey legs. The legs are big enough to satisfy some of the NFL linemen who can be found playing down the street at the gargantuan Cowboys Stadium.

Nolan Ryan notches his 5,000th strikeout (opposite). Texas Speedway (top) and the Sixth Floor Museum (above).

PLANES, TRAINS & AUTOMOBILES
Arlington is located about halfway between Dallas and Fort Worth and is a considerable distance from DFW International Airport. Rangers Ballpark is situated in an office park and, although relatively new, is one of the last of the subur-ban ballparks in the Majors. This is one town where driving is a must.

The four-story office structure located beyond the center-field wall is one of the signature features of the ballpark. It houses retail shops and the club's offices. Sports Park is an interactive area located in Vandergriff Plaza behind center field that includes a Wiffle ball park, tee-ball cages and picnic tables. Fans may also catch a glimpse of first-ballot Hall of Famer Nolan Ryan, the current club president and also part owner, who can sometimes be spotted working at the ballpark.

DEEP IN THE HEART OF TEXAS

It has been nearly two decades since the innovative and fiery Bobby Valentine served as manager of the Texas Rangers, but his restaurant, Bobby V's Sports Gallery Cafe, which is located in Arlington, remains one of the best sports bars in Texas. The place is

covered with an impressive collection of baseball memorabilia that will hold any fan's attention for at least a few drinks, if not more.

Drive 45 miles northeast of Arlington, and you'll find the Rangers Double-A affiliate, the Frisco RoughRiders of the Texas League, who play at Dr. Pepper Ballpark. Visitors have been known to draw comparisons between the look and feel of the park — with its unique architecture and nine interconnected pavilions — and that of Churchill Downs, the site of the Kentucky Derby in Louisville, Ky.

Visiting sports fans also like to flock to Sparkman Hillscrest Memorial Park in Dallas. The cemetery serves as the final resting place of legendary Hall of Famer Mickey Mantle, as well as the former Dallas Cowboys head coach, Tom Landry.

WORTH THE TRIP

Arlington lies about midway between Forth Worth and downtown Dallas, two cities that offer up plenty of signature Texas sites.

The Sixth Floor Museum at Dealey Plaza in Dallas memorializes the site of the assassination of President John F. Kennedy in 1963, as well as the legacy that he left behind. Other worthwhile Dallas attractions include the Dallas World Aquarium, the Meadows Museum of art, the Dallas Arboretum and the city's Botanical Gardens.

Home to Texas Christian University and the Texas Motor Speedway, Fort Worth retains its heritage as a Western town founded on cattle, railroads and oil thanks to Sundance Square, Fort Worth Stockyards and a cultural district that celebrates the history of this great Western city. Fort Worth is one of just two places, along with Washington D.C., where U.S. currency is printed. Tours are available at the Bureau of Engraving and Printing.

Adrenaline junkies should check out local theme parks Zero Gravity Dallas and Six Flags Over Texas, the oldest of the Six Flags amusement parks. Six Flags is near Rangers Ballpark and features some of the most popular roller coasters and thrill rides in the country. The company's adjacent park, Six Flags Hurricane Harbor, is a water-themed attraction for those who want to cool off on a hot summer day.

River Legacy Park, located on 1,300 acres along the Trinity River in North Arlington, has hiking and biking trails, playground and picnic areas and lots of attractive foliage in season.

The late-night crowd heads to the West End, Deep Ellum, Lower Greenville and McKinley Avenue areas.

WHAT'S IN A NAME?
During the franchise's days in the nation's capital, the name Senators fit this club to a T. But a move to Texas necessitated a name change, and the name of the Lone Star State's legendary police force fit the bill — thus the Rangers were born.

Kenny Rogers celebrates the first perfect game in franchise history (above) at Rangers Ballpark in Arlington against the Angels in July 1994 — the same year that the team inaugurated the retro-style ballpark, still a fan-favorite.

chapter 2

the southwest

PHOENIX
SAN DIEGO
LOS ANGELES

Phoenix

Coarse Sagebrush, rolling tumbleweed and prickly cactus may not be what most baseball fans picture when they think of America's pastime, but innovative Major League executive Bill Veeck — best known for growing ivy on the walls of Wrigley Field, zany promotions and "exploding" scoreboards — didn't see the game like everyone else when he brought the Indians to Arizona for Spring Training in 1947.

VALLEY OF THE SUN

Played in lush, rambling parks in the Northeast and mid-Atlantic states, baseball was a pastoral game in its infancy during the end of the 19th century. By the early 20th century, as the Major Leagues took root in cities in those same regions, ballparks were often an oasis of greenery in increasingly urban settings. St. Louis was the westernmost outpost of the Major Leagues as the game established itself as America's pastime. But that all began to change when innovative Big League executive Bill Veeck relocated his Cleveland Indians to Tucson, Ariz., for Spring Training in 1947 and convinced Giants Owner Horace Stoneham to move his club's spring camp to Phoenix.

With the Orioles and Cubs also moving their training camps to Arizona, the spring league there was dubbed the Cactus League in 1954. By the 1980s, it had grown to include the Cubs, Giants, Indians, Brewers, Angels, A's, Padres and Mariners. With the Indians departing for Florida in 1993, there was concern that the Cactus League would crumble, but instead, the northern Phoenix suburb of Peoria opened a state-of-the-art complex for the Padres and Mariners. The two-teams-per-park model was replicated in Surprise, Goodyear and Glendale, drawing the Dodgers, Reds, Royals and Rangers from Florida. Even the Indians returned to Arizona in 2009.

The popularity of Spring Training in Arizona, especially the passionate following for the Cubs and Giants, bolstered the cause for Phoenix as an expansion city. Jerry Colangelo, the longtime CEO of the NBA's Phoenix Suns, spearheaded the effort to land the expansion team that became the Arizona Diamondbacks in 1998.

Colangelo hit the ground running, paying top dollar for free agents and overseeing the construction of Bank One Ballpark (now Chase Field). The D-backs reached the playoffs in just their second season and won the 2001 World Series in their fourth, behind the stellar pitching of Randy Johnson and Curt Schilling. Since claiming the game's top prize, the D-backs have stayed competitive — reaching the NLCS in 2007 — while retooling with a young roster led by slugger Mark Reynolds and outfielders Justin Upton and Chris Young.

SNAKE BITTEN

Phoenix is often referred to as "Los Angeles East" because of its well-toned and glitzy big-event vibe. This reputation is alive and well at Chase Field where a crowd full of tanned, well-dressed twentysomethings come out to see and to be seen during the baseball season.

With its early success, the Diamondbacks quickly built a strong following throughout the Southwest, even though many transplants and longtime Spring Training fans still have

PLANES, TRAINS & AUTOMOBILES

Sky Harbor Airport is conveniently located near Chase Field. In fact, when the roof is open, inbound travelers can get a spectacular aerial view of the park. With little public transportation available, and Valley attractions spread out, Phoenix is a rental car–only town.

The Giants were one of the first clubs to hold Spring Training in Phoenix (above), helping pave the way for the Diamondbacks and Chase Field (left).

loyalties to seasonal residents, such as the Cubs, Giants and Mariners.

Like the Tampa Bay Rays — their '98 expansion brethren who also play in a Spring Training hotbed — the D-backs have to worry about local fans suffering from baseball overload. Up to 15 clubs make their home in the Valley at some point during the year, with D-backs fans able to hop over to nearby Scottsdale to catch the team during Spring Training.

And as if this wasn't enough baseball, there's also the Arizona Fall League, which fields six teams of top prospects at five Spring Training sites during October and November. It's great baseball and offers fans a glimpse at the next generation of stars.

THE WILD WEST
When it opened in 1998, the D-backs' home became the model for new parks in warm climates, featuring real grass, a retractable roof and plenty of amenities to keep fans comfortable.

With temperatures soaring above 110 degrees in Phoenix during much of the season, it's often necessary to close the roof and crank up the 8,000-ton air conditioning system, which is strong enough to cool 2,500 single-family homes.

The west entrance of the park is a rotunda that pays tribute to Brooklyn's Ebbets Field. There are plenty of activities for the kids, too, including an arcade in the outfield and a mini-field where toddlers can play. Then there's the ballpark's most famous feature — the swimming pool beyond center field that is available for group rentals.

The Diamondbacks followed the example of Coors Field in Denver and Turner Field in Atlanta with a wide-open lower level that enables fans to keep watching the game even while waiting in line for concessions.

Chase Field's signature dish is the Arizona Dog, a foot-long hot dog topped with spicy chorizo sausage, nacho cheese and crunchy corn tortilla strips. Chase Field's frozen drinks are also a welcome treat on a hot summer day. The young, professional crowd tends to flock to adjacent bars such as Sliders and Hi Tops, both two stories tall and located just outside the ballpark.

DESERT BLOOM
While diamond devotees will want to visit most Big League cities during the season, Arizona might actually be the most desirable location for a road trip before Opening Day when the proximity of Spring Training sites makes it possible to catch two games a day in March.

Baseball fans should not miss Don & Charlie's Steakhouse in Scottsdale. Decorated from floor to ceiling with sports memorabilia, it's a popular gathering spot for baseball insiders, especially during Spring Training.

Arizona State University, alma mater of Reggie Jackson, Barry Bonds and Dustin Pedroia — and home to the mighty Sun Devils baseball program — plays its home games in the heart of ASU's campus, in nearby Tempe.

SOUTHWESTERN SIGHTS

With 300-plus days of sunshine per year, Phoenix showcases some of the most beautiful landscaping, golf courses and resorts in the country. Few other areas offer as many ways to explore, whether via hot air balloon, Jeep tour, hiking, biking, horseback riding or mountain climbing.

Many visitors to Phoenix head directly for the red rocks of Sedona, located two hours to the north. Some trek even further afield to the Grand Canyon, which sits about four hours north of the city. Both are worth the trip, although there's plenty to experience in the greater Phoenix area itself.

Tops on the list of Phoenix's must-see sights are the Desert Botanical Gardens, which display more than 20,000 desert plants from around the world and are also adjacent to the Phoenix Zoo. Two museums that are unique to Phoenix are the downtown Heard Museum, one of the nation's most comprehensive museums of Native American culture; and Taliesin West, which was built as a winter retreat by Frank Lloyd Wright in 1937. The latter now serves as the headquarters of the Frank Lloyd Wright Foundation and School of Architecture.

The Mill Avenue district of shops and restaurants is fun to visit while at ASU, especially for some happening nightlife. Just north of Tempe is Old Town Scottsdale. With its many souvenir shops and kitschy attractions, it's worth making the trip, even if crowds of tourists are the norm. Just west of Scottsdale Road, the Scottsdale Art District is full of galleries. It's also home to the area's liveliest and most exclusive nightclubs.

WHAT'S IN A NAME?

Looking for a name with bite, Arizona turned the designation of its 1998 expansion team over to fans. While Scorpions and Coyotes were in the hunt, Arizonans looked to the venomous rattlesnake — specifically the pattern on its back — for final inspiration, combining local wildlife and baseball references to hatch their fearsome Diamondbacks.

Arizona's landscape is perfect for exploring (opposite). Randy Johnson (above) won four straight Cy Young Awards with the D-backs, and led them to the 2001 World Series title.

San Diego

With ideal weather nearly year-round, San Diego's baseball roots go back more than a century, even if the city is a relative newcomer to Major League Baseball — the Padres didn't debut until 1969. The first professional game in San Diego took place on Nov. 13, 1887, when the touring Philadelphia Phillies routed a team of locals, 31-7. Despite the rough start, the city has since produced some of the game's best.

MAJOR LEAGUE MISSIONARIES

Fans plotting a course to Petco Park in San Diego should take note of the Padres' location: bordered on the south and west by Tony Gwynn Drive. A native of Southern California and the current baseball coach at San Diego State University, Gwynn spent every season of his 20-year Hall of Fame career with the Padres, notching 3,141 hits and helping the club reach the World Series in 1984 and 1998.

"One of the things I'm proudest about is that I played for one team. My baseball card looks awesome because it has San Diego all the way down," Gwynn has said. "I grew up in an environment where that kind of stuff was important. Loyalty was a small part of it. It was a matter of it being comfortable, of being in a place where I could do what I did without a lot of external pressure. This was just the place."

With all due respect to Gwynn and his eight National League batting titles, Ted Williams is San Diego's most acclaimed baseball personality, and his alma mater, Hoover High, plays its games on Ted Williams Field. The "Splendid Splinter" debuted with the Pacific Coast League's San Diego Padres as a 17-year-old in 1937.

In the 1920s, baseball was played at Balboa Stadium, which was a football field on the campus of San Diego High, measuring just 250 feet down the line in left. The short dimensions must have tempted Babe Ruth and Lou Gehrig to push one to the opposite field during an exhibition game played at the field in 1927.

Sports Field, a multipurpose venue that hosted football, baseball and motorcycle events, was remodeled as Lane Field in the 1930s when Bill Lane moved his Hollywood franchise of the Pacific Coast League. Constructed largely of wood and built at the end of West Broadway near the waterfront, Lane Field suffered from termite infestation and moisture damage. It was also the place where locals got their first glimpse of Williams during his days with the Minor League Padres. In 1957, the club moved north to Mission Valley, which later housed the National League version of the Padres at Jack Murphy Stadium (later known as Qualcomm Stadium). In 2004, the Padres returned to downtown San Diego, opening Petco Park not far from the site of Lane Field. As the Padres prepared to open their new digs, they made sure to honor Gwynn.

PADRE FAMILIAS

A California native, Major Leaguer and Marine pilot in World War II and the Korean War, broadcaster Jerry Coleman was the conduit between generations of Padres fans and the local nine. His malaprops and enthusiasm endeared him to fans, who in turn came to treat the franchise like family — you loved them even during the tough times.

Although the Padres embarked on a magical run to the 1984 World Series — perhaps inspired by the death of longtime Owner Ray Kroc — and treated fans to Tony Gwynn's steady march to 3,000 hits and the Hall of Fame, it wasn't until John Moores purchased the club following the 1994 season that the franchise managed to consistently give fans an exciting ballclub to support. To compete with the countless recreational activities available in the San Diego area, Moores opened beautiful Petco Park in 2004 and created the most fan-friendly, customer-service oriented team in baseball. The organizational attitude didn't change when ownership passed to former agent Jeff Moorad.

With the Marine Corps, Navy and Coast Guard all having large numbers of personnel stationed in San Diego, it's not unusual to see uniformed men and women in the stands at Petco Park. In deference to the team's brave and patriotic fans, the Padres don camouflage alternate uniforms for all Sunday home games.

PICTURE PERFECT

The friendliness and customer service provided by Padres employees are nearly as sunny as the weather in San Diego, and both add up to a very pleasant fan experience for visitors of Petco Park.

PLANES, TRAINS & AUTOMOBILES

There's plenty to see and do just by strolling the downtown Gaslamp Quarter District — the trolley conveniently stops near Petco Park. Still, residents tend to follow the car culture of Southern California. The traffic isn't quite as bad as it is in Los Angeles, and most visitors rent cars to explore the beaches as well as the attractions in northern San Diego County.

Tony Gwynn (left) spent his Major League career in San Diego, where SeaWorld (top) and the San Diego Zoo (above) are top draws.

Larry Lucchino, the team's president from 1995 to 2001, helped design Baltimore's Camden Yards and worked diligently to bring an even better park to San Diego. Instead of the green seats and red brick so typical of Orioles Park and its successors, Petco features blue seats, stucco and Indian sandstone that better fit the atmosphere of the coastal city.

Petco also features the closest thing to Baltimore's signature B&O Warehouse. The century-old Western Metal Supply Co. building was scheduled for demolition before Petco architects incorporated it into the design of the ballpark. The renovated building contains the team store, private suites and a restaurant.

The ballpark itself has some of the game's most breathtaking scenery, with views of the San Diego Bay and Balboa Park beyond center field. Just past the outfield fence is a 2.7-acre "Park at the Park," which serves as an open green during non-event hours and provides affordable seating during games. The area includes a Little League infield, kids' play area and a statue of Tony Gwynn.

Petco Park arguably has the best food selection in all of baseball, with Southwest and Mexican offerings served alongside traditional ballpark fare. The Padres are famous for their fish tacos, a San Diego specialty. Randy Jones BBQ, created by the former Padres pitcher who won the '76 National League Cy Young Award, is known for its pork and Jones' signature barbecue sauce — which can also be found at local grocery stores.

SHIPS AND SHAMU

Downtown San Diego is quite impressive without being imposing. The 130-block East Village is the largest neighborhood, while the Gaslamp Quarter District is the city's historic area, with more than 100 restaurants plus plenty of nightclubs and bars.

Downtown San Diego is also home to the USS Midway Museum, where visitors can tour the longest-serving aircraft carrier in U.S. Navy history. Twenty-five aircrafts rest on the ship's 1,001-foot runway. Flight simulators below deck give visitors the chance to be a pilot, even if just for a few minutes.

Nearby Balboa Park is one of San Diego's most popular destinations, with more than 1,200 acres of museums, performing arts venues and gardens.

Of course, San Diego is home to SeaWorld, where you can catch a performance by the city's biggest star, Shamu the killer whale. There's the world-famous San Diego Zoo, the Reuben H. Fleet Science Center and 15 museums, including the San Diego Air & Space Museum and the San Diego Hall of Champions Sports Museum.

About 20 miles north of San Diego, the city of Carlsbad offers many family attractions, including Legoland California, a theme park based entirely on the beloved plastic building blocks. The Flower Fields of Carlsbad is a 50-acre hillside nursery of flowers that bloom in spectacular color each spring, just in time for Opening Day.

The USS Midway Museum (above) offers tours and flight simulations and is one of many non-baseball attractions that fans should visit while in San Diego, in addition to catching a Padres game at beautiful Petco Park (opposite).

Los Angeles

Whether enraptured by the silver screen, surf or Disneyland, Americans have looked to Southern California to make their dreams come true — or at least to provide refuge from the dreary winters elsewhere. With balmy days at the beach and exciting nightlife, where the stars in the sky are jealous of those in the Hollywood Hills, Los Angeles and Anaheim bring a totally different flavor to any Major League road trip.

WEST SIDE STORY

The history of baseball in Southern California can be traced through the caps of the top teams. From 1903–57, the Los Angeles Angels were one of the dominant clubs in the Pacific Coast League, winning the pennant 11 times. Los Angeles County fielded a second PCL team, the Vernon Tigers, from 1909–25. As he prepared to move his Brooklyn Dodgers west, O'Malley purchased the Angels early in 1957 and moved the team north to Spokane, Wash., the following year. The Angels' cap — navy blue with a red "A" — was tweaked to the Dodgers' signature shade of blue and embossed with the white "LA" logo. Although Walter O'Malley was vilified by Brooklynites for taking their beloved "Bums," the Dodgers were welcomed in Los Angeles with open arms. They won the World Series in 1959, just their second season on the West Coast.

In 1961, several groups, including one headed by Hall of Famers Hank Greenberg and Bill Veeck, made bids for the new American League franchise slated to play in Los Angeles. Gene Autry, the actor, "singing cowboy" and owner of the Hollywood Stars of the Pacific Coast League, initially wanted only the team's broadcast rights but was persuaded to take charge of the entire organization. He became one of the most beloved owners in baseball history, and the Angels doffed red caps with a white "A."

Autry's club — first named the Los Angeles Angels but rechristened the California Angels in 1965 — began play in 1961 at a Minor League park and then played four seasons in Dodger Stadium until the team's ballpark in Anaheim was ready for the 1966 campaign.

The Angels did not reach the postseason until 1979 and generally played in the shadows of the mighty Dodgers until Mike Scioscia took over as skipper in 2000 and turned the team into a perennial contender. The Dodgers, erstwhile, thrived during Tommy Lasorda's 20-year run as manager, reaching the World Series four times and winning titles in 1981 and 1988. In 2008, Joe Torre took the helm after a long, successful run with the Yankees and lifted the Dodgers back into contention in the Senior Circuit.

PLANES, TRAINS & AUTOMOBILES

Although Los Angeles has the most devoted automobile culture in the nation, there is train service to Angels Stadium and bus service to Dodger Stadium. The freeways are notoriously congested, but they're still the easiest way to get to all of the many far-flung beaches and attractions in Los Angeles and its surrounding counties.

The Angels and Dodgers aren't the only stars in Southern California.

HEAVEN SENT

In the early 1990s, sportswriter Steve Rushin wore an Angels cap as he traveled through California, reporting on the fan experience at every single ballpark for a *Sports Illustrated* article. Rushin marveled that the Angels hat generated no remarks. Apparently, nobody felt passionately about the "other" Los Angeles team.

Within a decade that had changed dramatically. Between the extreme makeover of Angel Stadium in the late '90s, the Angels' run of AL West dominance — highlighted by the 2002 World Series triumph — and the fan-friendly ownership of Arte Moreno, the team has developed a rabid following. These days, fans create a sea of red at the "Big A" to rival that of Cardinals fans at Busch Stadium.

It helps that the Angels have been one of more successful teams of the new millennium, which began with the appointment of Mike Scioscia as manager. The Philadelphia native and ex-Dodgers catcher brought a relentless work ethic to the club, and fans have responded. Whether it was the riotous din created by Thunderstix or the cheers that greeted the Rally Monkey whenever he appeared on the Jumbotron, Angels fans have been eager to embrace the next big thing when it comes to rooting on the home team.

'A' PLUS

Those who know Angel Stadium only from its cameo in *The Naked Gun* may do a double take upon arriving at the park in Anaheim. The extensive renovation of a former multipurpose stadium in 1997–98 resulted in essentially a new ballpark at the same site.

The landmark "Big A" sign and electronic marquee, once part of the scoreboard, is now on display in the parking lot. Architects took a vast concrete facility and gave it the feel of a freshly-designed ballpark. There are courtyards with palm trees and a main entry plaza complete with giant bats

WHAT'S IN A NAME?

Previously a Minor League ballclub in the Chicago Cubs farm system, a group of Angels played their first season at a West Coast Wrigley Field. After moving to Anaheim and setting up camp on Dodger turf in 1966, franchise patriarch Gene Autry made sure the expansion team proudly donned a name (since 1961) with which the City of Angels could connect.

From the charming Gene Autry (opposite, second from right) to the Rally Monkey (above), the "Big A" has been home to all sorts of characters over the years.

and batting helmets. Inside, the park offers unobstructed concourses and clear sightlines. The signature "Outfield Extravaganza," located beyond the center-field wall, was built to replicate the rocky and scenic California coastline. It brings the park to life with a 90-foot geyser and pyrotechnics whenever a special moment takes place on the field.

THINK BLUE

Dodgers fans have long been known to arrive fashionably late and to leave early to beat the notorious L.A. traffic. Such grousing could be the result of an unfair comparison to the legendary Ebbets Field devotees of the club. In reality, fans at Chavez Ravine have long embraced the Dodgers, who have ranked among the National League attendance leaders since arriving in Los Angeles in 1958. Part of the reason the bond between the team and the fanbase grew so quickly is Dodgers announcer Vin Scully, a franchise cornerstone with the ability to make each broadcast feel like a family chat at the dinner table. Peter O'Malley worked to foster a family relationship between the franchise and its fans after his father moved the club across the country.

Dodgers fans tend to have the California-cool mentality and, like the international flavor of the Dodgers roster, they're a diverse group akin to players like Jackie Robinson, Hideo Nomo, Orel Hershiser and Manny Ramirez. It's not just Tommy Lasorda who bleeds Dodger

WHAT'S IN A NAME?
During the late 19th century, Brooklyn was a maze of interlocking, crisscrossing trolley lines. Brooklynites traveling on foot were left to constantly dodge the trains, earning the nickname "Trolley Dodgers." After using the name on and off for several decades, the team adopted the Dodgers nickname for good in 1932, eventually bringing it to Los Angeles.

Tommy Lasorda (far left) is still beloved by Dodgers fans years after his retirement.

Although glitzy Rodeo Drive in Beverly Hills (right) — with its upscale shopping and celeb sightings — may seem a quintessential Los Angeles experience, coming out to Chavez Ravine (top) — and imitating Manny Ramirez — can't be left off any traveler's to-do list.

blue. You're more likely to see celebrities at Dodger Stadium than in any other ballpark, but despite a reputation for coming to be seen, most Dodgers fans arrive to be part of one of baseball's great communities.

OLD SCHOOL

From Dodgertown in Vero Beach, Fla., to Ebbets Field on Flatbush Avenue in Brooklyn, the Dodgers have always been synonymous with great baseball destinations, and Dodger Stadium is no exception. It resides in Chavez Ravine, one of the most idyllic settings in the Majors. The ballpark provides breathtaking views of the surrounding San Gabriel Mountains and the Elysian Hills through a wide opening between the decks in left and right field.

With a little help from a 2006 renovation, Dodger Stadium has stood the test of time, still retaining its old-school charm. There are no modern gimmicks, no sprawling sports bars or club levels. There's just baseball, presented pretty much the same way since the building opened in 1962. For some fans, it might not be as hallowed as Wrigley Field or Fenway, the game's only older parks, but Dodger Stadium offers a better view and more legroom than the other two.

It also offers Dodger Dogs, perhaps the most famous baseball food. Nearly a foot long, the hot dogs are served boiled or grilled depending on the concession stand. If you want to blend in with the other Angelenos, grab the grilled style — it's still considered the true original.

STARS AND STUDENTS

The University of Southern California's baseball team is a perennial powerhouse and the alma mater of many legendary Major Leaguers, including Tom Seaver, Randy Johnson, Mark McGwire and Barry Zito.

Overall, the area is one of the most fertile in the country for college baseball. Other talent-laden schools include UCLA, Cal State Fullerton and UC Irvine. The Fullerton campus is just a few minutes north of Angel Stadium.

To offer respect to the game's past, head to Inglewood Park Cemetery and

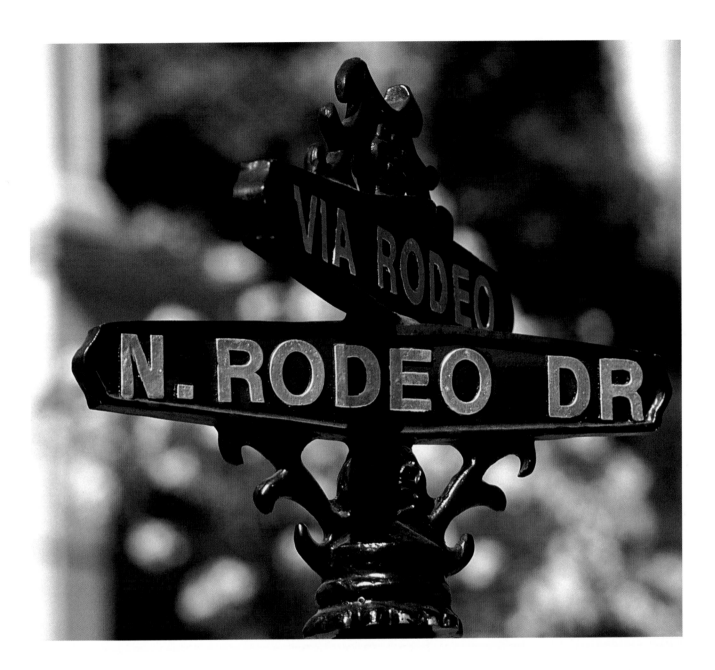

pay tribute to former stars including Hall of Famers Sam Crawford and Bobby Wallace, as well as Wally Berger, Lyman Bostock, Curt Flood and Jim Gilliam. Baseball icons have also claimed several stars on the Hollywood Walk of Fame, including former Angels Owner Gene Autry and Chuck Connors, who played in both the Major Leagues and the NBA and starred in the hit 1950s TV series *The Rifleman*.

LA-LA LAND

Whether you enjoy theme parks, stargazing in Hollywood, relaxing at the beach, taking in arts and culture, hiking or exploring the desert, there's always something to do in Southern California, which encompasses Orange, Ventura and Riverside counties.

Los Angeles is one of the few cities where All-Stars may be overshadowed by people in the stands. But with both teams playing in Hollywood's back-yard, visitors at Angels and Dodgers games might end up sitting next to a sitcom star. It's also possible to stargaze at the beach, while window shopping on high-end Rodeo Drive, or by taking bus tours of celebrity estates. For a real taste of fame, head to one of Beverly Hills' exquisite restaurants — where many renowned celebrity chefs turn out culinary delights.

Other star attractions include the Greek Theater and the Hollywood Walk of Fame. Visitors with kids in tow — or who remain young at heart — place Disneyland on the top of their to-do list in Orange County. The theme park is just down Katella Avenue from Angel Stadium. Many fans enjoy Mickey during the day and the Angels at night.

Also check out the Knott's Berry Farm theme park in Buena Park, with its old-fashioned roller coasters and great dining. Some of the nation's most upscale beach communities are in striking distance of Anaheim, including Newport Beach, Dana Point, Laguna Beach and Huntington Beach.

chapter 3

the northwest

BAY AREA
SEATTLE
DENVER

Bay Area

From Cy Young Award–winning, long-haired Giants pitching prodigy Tim Lincecum to the Athletics' unkempt, bombastic championship-winning clubs of the 1970s, San Francisco and Oakland have fielded iconoclastic stars through the years, befitting the Bay Area's well-known reputation as a counterculture haven. Both Big League clubs have used brains and brawn to stay ahead of the competition.

TAKING SIDES

Under traditional circumstances, a meeting between two local rivals polarizes a community. Yet the entire Bay Area came together during the 1989 Fall Classic between the San Francisco Giants and Oakland Athletics, due to the devastating Loma Prieta Earthquake. The 15-second quake was caused by a slip along the San Andreas Fault, which runs throughout California. It struck on Oct. 17, 1989 at 5:04 p.m., as the teams were preparing for Game 3 of the "Battle of the Bay" at Candlestick Park in San Francisco. Television viewers around the country, however, were listening to broadcaster Tim McCarver recount highlights from the first two games of the Series, not officially learning of the quake until 5:40 PM.

Since the ballpark sustained no damage, everyone inside was slow to realize the extent of the wreckage outside, but it was only a matter of time before word reached the players and fans. The violent tremor caused a 50-foot section of the Bay Bridge to break off and forced the collapse of the two-level Cypress Street Viaduct of Interstate 880 in West Oakland. Before play resumed 10 days later, Oakland ace and Bay Area native Dave Stewart helped gather food for workers and clothing for displaced families. Upon the Series' return, the A's completed a four-game sweep, their only Series win in three straight Fall Classic appearances (1988–90).

For more than a century leading up to the Series, the two cities had a sibling rivalry. The San Francisco Seals and Oakland Oaks played key roles in the Pacific Coast League, which began in 1903. Thanks to California's warm weather, PCL teams played marathon seasons, even eclipsing 200 games in early years. From 1926–37, the league included a second San Francisco team, the Mission Reds, sometimes called simply the "Missions" after the working-class Mission District.

In 1932, Seals outfielder Vince DiMaggio arranged a tryout for his younger brother, Joe. The DiMaggio brothers grew up in San Francisco, and would have followed their father into the fishing industry had baseball not beckoned. The year after his tryout, Joe joined the Seals and hit safely in 61 consecutive games.

The Giants arrived in San Francisco in 1958 and, after finishing sixth in each of their last two years in New York, put up 14 consecutive winning seasons, thanks in part to future Hall of Famers Willie Mays, Juan Marichal and Willie McCovey.

The Giants' streak ended in 1972. But by then the A's — who had arrived in neighboring Oakland from Kansas City for the 1968 season — had begun a five-year postseason stretch that would produce three consecutive

World Series titles (1972–74). Despite having lost players to free agency in the late 1970s, and their relatively small payroll, the Athletics remained a consistently strong team for decades, ensuring that there was at least one contender in the Bay Area at any given time.

LARGER THAN LIFE

When the Giants headed west to Northern California in the late 1950s, the franchise came with a ready-made superstar in Willie Mays and a natural geographic rival in the Los Angeles Dodgers, giving local fans a team to cheer for *and* a team to root against.

Mays was eventually joined by homegrown stars Willie McCovey and Bobby Bonds and Dominican ace Juan Marichal. With so many All-Star–caliber players in the franchise's early years in San Francisco, the only thing for fans to complain about was chilly, blustery Candlestick Park. Even the occasional Giants player let it be known that he didn't care too much for the club's drafty home field.

PLANES, TRAINS & AUTOMOBILES

The Bay Area Rapid Transit system — known to locals as BART— is a convenient way to get around San Francisco, Oakland and the surrounding areas. The system connects to both the newly expanded Oakland International Airport, which is minutes from the A's ballpark, and the San Francisco International Airport.

With multiple bus, streetcar, metro and ferry options, there's no need to drive to AT&T Park for a Giants game or to Oakland-Alameda County Coliseum. But if you have a car, Oakland's stadium has plenty of space for parking.

The Bay Bridge (right) connects San Francisco with nearby Oakland and provides the backdrop for the San Francisco Giants' picturesque AT&T Park.

After a lean run through the 1980s, five-tool superstar Barry Bonds and skipper Dusty Baker arrived in 1993, and Giants fans were coming out en masse again. With the club's move into a brand spanking new home in 2000, the Giants were re-energized. Bonds thrilled fans with his run for the all-time home run record and led the club to three NL West titles and the 2002 NL pennant.

BY THE BAYSIDE

After years of battling the swirling winds at Candlestick Park, Giants players and fans were blessed with AT&T Park in 2000. Along with Pittsburgh's PNC Park, the facility may be the top of the line in terms of the new generation of modern stadiums.

There's the classic architecture highlighted by a pair of 112-foot King Street clock towers, each topped by a 45-foot flagpole. There's the statue of Giants Hall of Famer Willie Mays at the ballpark's main entrance. There are the breathtaking waterfront views and the intoxicating scents of garlic fries and crab cake sandwiches. And of course, there are the constant upgrades that tech-savvy Giants have made since the park opened at the turn of the 21st century.

Perhaps best of all is McCovey Cove, just beyond the right-field fence, where adventurous fans, often armed with nets, float in kayaks and small boats in the hope of catching a home run ball. No ballpark better blends a city's geography, history, cuisine, personality and industry than AT&T Park.

A-OK

Although A's fans don't fit neatly into any box, they have often seemed to follow suit with the players of the time. In the early '70s, fans and players were often seen sporting the same long-haired style that reflected both the time and the counterculture attitude of Northern California. They carried them-

Whether taking to the waters of McCovey Cove beyond the right-field wall at AT&T Park (left) to wait for a home run ball or crowding around Willie Mays (above) in search of an autograph, Giants fans have always been an intrepid group.

selves with bravado as Sal Bando and Reggie Jackson led the team to three titles in a row, and again from 1988–90 when the "Bash Brothers" — sluggers Mark McGwire and Jose Canseco — reached the World Series three consecutive times, winning in 1989.

In the new millennium, A's fans have reveled in the club's role as the resourceful upstart David that was capable of toppling the big-market Goliaths. From 1999–2006, Billy Beane's *Moneyball* A's won four AL West titles, while exploiting inefficiencies in the way big-spending rivals construct rosters.

AN INTIMATE AFFAIR

Oakland-Alameda County Coliseum was long considered one of the more beautiful multi-sport stadiums. The park's panoramic views of the Oakland hills have served as a postcard-perfect backdrop since its opening in 1968.

When 10,000 seats were added in 1996 as a condition of Raiders Owner Al Davis moving his NFL franchise back to Oakland, the stadium was enclosed and the view was blocked. To recapture the cozier atmosphere, the A's have placed tarps on some of the upper-deck seating in recent years, reducing capacity to 35,067 for regular-season games. On the bright side, the park's vast size means food options are plentiful.

The smaller capacity provides a comfortable, relaxed ballpark experience, and the Athletics have made their home family friendly. The A's mascot, Stomper the elephant, makes his way around the ballpark throughout every game. There's the Stomper Fun Zone, located on the club concourse behind section 220, where kids can enjoy a Speed Pitch game, rides and interactive attractions.

WHAT'S IN A NAME?

When the Philadelphia Athletics were founded in 1901, they took their name from the Philadelphia Athletic Club. The team moved to Kansas City before heading to its final stop, Oakland, but through the years the club has always been known as the Athletics.

Reggie Jackson and Rollie Fingers (above, from left) were a huge part of the A's success during the early '70s. Stomper greets fans at Oakland-Alameda County Coliseum (right).

MEET ME HALFWAY

From Alcatraz in the middle of the bay to the Golden Gate Bridge, Lombard Street, Chinatown and Fisherman's Wharf, the Bay Area is a treat for first-timers as well as veteran visitors.

Although San Francisco is one of the top cities to explore by foot, don't miss

riding one of the famous cable cars as well — they're considered moving landmarks. San Francisco has more than 40 hills — including the famed Twin Peaks, but also Mount Davidson, Bernal Heights and Tank Hill. Those who make it to the top of Coit Tower are treated to a bird's-eye view of the city.

For a timeless San Francisco experience, head to Union Square, one of the city's three original parks. It's now a prime shopping district with upscale shops and hotels, mere steps from the theater district.

Oakland often gets overshadowed by its cosmopolitan neighbor, but this Northern California treasure has plenty

of its own attractions. Lake Merritt is the largest man-made salt-water lake in an urban area, covering 155 acres and surrounded by parks and trails. Just off of its shores is the nation's first theme park, Children's Fairyland. Perfect for the younger set, the amusement park has rides like the famous

Spiderweb Ferris Wheel and the less-scary Jolly Trolly.

Head to the shores of the Bay to check out Jack London Square. It's home to plenty of shops, restaurants and the historic Heinold's First and Last Chance Saloon. For late night action, listen to some blues at the Fox Theater.

The San Francisco Giants warm up before the '89 World Series in Oakland.

Seattle

Nestled along Puget Sound, Seattle has had its fortunes rise and fall with the tides for generations. Its populace has been at home on the water — and, perhaps not coincidentally, in the rain. Dubbed "Rain City," this metropolis in the heart of the Pacific Northwest offers a peek at a maritime way of life unfamiliar in most of the country, and a ballclub that's fittingly dubbed the Mariners.

THE EMERALD CITY

The multipurpose Kingdome, with its expansive foul territory and obscured views, was certainly not as fan-friendly as Safeco Field, but the original home of the Seattle Mariners was the site of the wildest and most exciting game in franchise history. With the 1995 American League Division Series between the M's and the New York Yankees tied at two games apiece, 57,411 fans cheered as the home team came from behind in the bottom of the 11th inning and toppled the Bronx Bombers in the decisive fifth game.

With Joey Cora and Ken Griffey Jr. on base, Edgar Martinez doubled on a liner to left. Cora scored and Griffey came charging after him. The superstar center fielder slid safely, and delirium ensued as the Mariners celebrated their biggest win in club history.

Watching Griffey being mobbed by his teammates in front of a football-stadium-sized crowd, it would be easy to forget the franchise's humble beginnings. The city responsible for meteoric success stories — Starbucks, Microsoft, Amazon.com and grunge rock, for example — took a little bit longer to establish itself as a Major League Baseball hotbed.

The Seattle Indians, later known as the Angels and more famously as the Rainiers, were charter members of the Pacific Coast League. The Emerald City's team competed in the PCL from 1903–06 and 1919–68, and also in the Northwest League. Seattle received an American League expansion team for 1971, but the timetable was moved up to 1969 to appease Kansas City officials, who were also awarded a team and didn't want to wait long to replace the A's, who left for Oakland after the '67 season.

The Seattle Pilots debuted along with the Royals, Montreal Expos and San Diego Padres. Unfortunately, the Pilots' ownership was woefully undercapitalized and the

PLANES, TRAINS & AUTOMOBILES

Since Seattle is isolated from most of the country, plane tickets can be expensive. Safeco Field and many of Seattle's attractions are within close proximity to downtown, making buses an attractive option throughout the metro area. There is also a frequent and reliable streetcar line running through downtown. But many visitors, having made the odyssey to Seattle, tend to rent cars and explore the surrounding areas, sometimes even venturing north to Vancouver.

Ichiro Suzuki's consistent hitting and solid defense has won him just as much adoration in Seattle as in his native Japan, where he played for nine years prior to joining the Mariners.

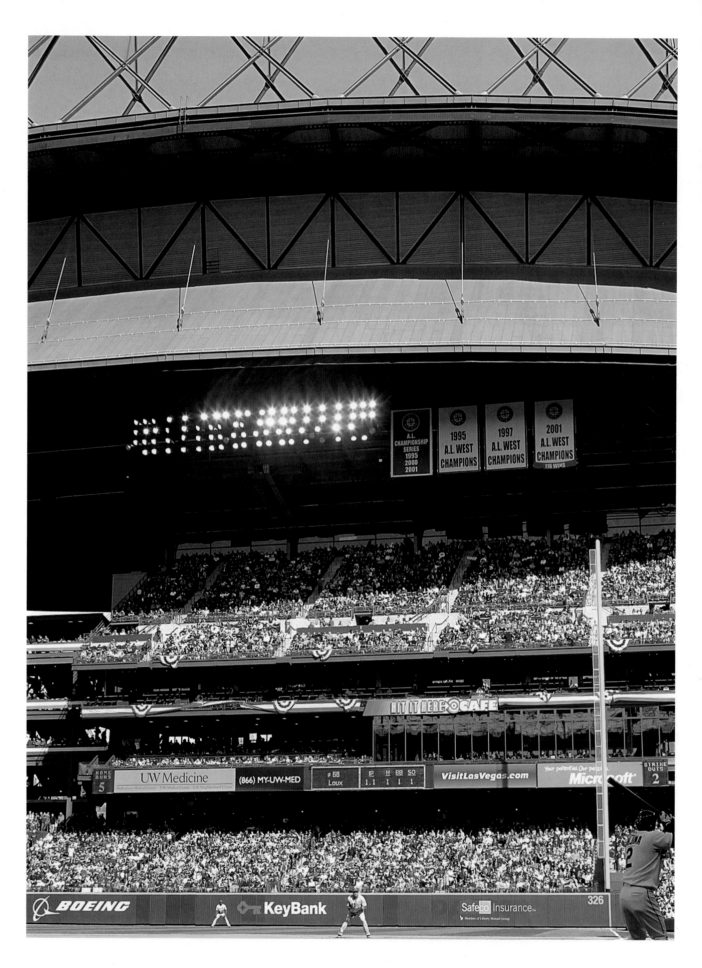

team won a lowly 64 games at tiny Sicks Stadium, drawing just 677,000 fans in its inaugural campaign. After that season, the Pilots owners sold the club to a group led by future Commissioner of Baseball Bud Selig, who moved the team to Milwaukee.

Upset over the loss of its Major League team, the City of Seattle sued the American League for breach of contract, and was awarded the Mariners, who debuted in 1977. Playing in the Kingdome along with the NFL's Seahawks, the Mariners didn't get off to a much better start than the Pilots.

Things changed in the 1990s, when Lou Piniella managed one of the game's most beloved teams — a group including Griffey, Martinez, Randy Johnson and Alex Rodriguez. Including the spirited '95 run to the ALCS, the Mariners reached the playoffs four times in a seven-year span that included the opening of a new ballpark, Safeco Field, in 1999. As the 1990s assemblage of stars scattered due to retirement and free agency, Ichiro Suzuki arrived from Japan, leading the team to 116 wins in 2001 and enrapturing fans at Safeco — and back home — with his endless stream of hits and stolen bases.

SEA-ING BLUE AND GREEN
Although Seattle will always remain enamored with the 1995 "Refuse to Lose" club that featured Ken Griffey Jr., Edgar Martinez, Randy Johnson and Jay Buhner — stars who took the team to its first playoff appearance in franchise history — local fans also seem to appreciate younger, lesser-known ballplayers who are just beginning to emerge. Potentially a by-product of the club's leaner early years, the mindset to stick with youngsters paid dividends in 2001 when, with the exception of Buhner and Martinez, the aforementioned stars had been replaced by a wave of fresh, new talent who arrived on the shores of the Pacific Northwest.

But the fans came out to the beautiful new park in droves, and skipper Lou Piniella won an AL-record 116 games with a rookie named Ichiro leading the club after Johnson, Griffey and Co. had moved on. The city embraced the

idiosyncratic Japanese import and a bunch of low-wattage grinders from whom little was expected. Maybe it was the crash of the first Internet gold rush, sending Microsoft stock tumbling, that made fans appreciate blue-collar players not looking for a big payday out of town. Whatever the reason, fans never wavered, and their faith was rewarded with a landmark season.

SAFE-TY FIRST
In the rain-dappled Pacific Northwest, Safeco Field manages the trick of being an open-air venue while still protecting fans from the elements. The stadium features a one-of-a-kind retractable roof designed to cover but not enclose the ballpark, thus preserving the open-air environment.

Inside Safeco, you'll find the Baseball Museum of the Pacific Northwest —

home to the Mariners Hall of Fame. Bring young fans to the "Moose Den" in center, where they can meet the Mariner Moose. Original baseball-themed art is also scattered throughout the park.

WHAT'S IN A NAME?
The latest Seattle franchise joined the Major Leagues during the 1977 expansion, and like so many others, the owners held a contest to name the team. The people spoke, choosing the Mariners, which paid tribute to "the natural association between the sea and Seattle and her people."

Opening Day '09 at Safeco Field (left) matched the M's against the Los Angeles Angels. The Space Needle (above) was originally built for the 1962 World's Fair.

Safeco features many restaurants and food options and has been recognized by ESPN and the Food Network for its culinary offerings. Instead of limiting itself to standard ballpark fare, the Mariners feature local vendors who serve everything from pad Thai, chicken teriyaki and strawberries on a stick to the popular garlic fries. Don't miss Ivar's, a famous Seattle eatery that has six locations at Safeco, which serves grilled wild-caught salmon sandwiches and other seafood delicacies such as the famous Ichiroll — a tuna sushi with sesame flakes named just for Seattle's Japanese All-Star.

GATEWAY TO THE PACIFIC

The Pike Place Market is one of the oldest continuously operated farmer's markets in North America. Built into a steep hill and spread over a nine-acre historic district in the heart of downtown, it has several lower levels with arts and crafts, ethnic groceries and gift stores, vintage clothing, antiques and collectibles, international restaurants and cafes. The street level is home to produce stands and the world-famous Pike Place Fish Market, where employees throw three-foot salmon and other fish to each other rather than simply passing

them by hand. The maritime history of Seattle comes alive watching the fishmongers at work, making the local baseball team's name seem even more spot-on.

Seattle's historic district, located on the southern fringe of the downtown business area, features 20 square blocks of picturesque Victorian Romanesque architecture, museums, many art galleries, plus a slew of unique restaurants and nightclubs. The historic 5th Avenue Theatre was built in 1926, and still regularly stages Broadway-style musical shows featuring both local talent and international stars.

The legacy of the 1962 Seattle World's Fair, Seattle Center, is a 74-acre park that's home to the instantly recognizable 605-foot Space Needle. Many visits to Seattle often begin with a trip to the Needle's observation tower, which provides the most dramatic view of the city. The Pacific Science Center, Science Fiction Museum and Hall of Fame, Experience Music Project, Seattle Opera, Intiman Playhouse, Pacific Northwest Ballet, Seattle Repertory Theatre, Seattle Children's Theatre and the Seattle Children's Museum are also there, providing enough entertainment for an entire week's trip.

Pike Place Market (left) serves up fresh fish in addition to myriad gifts, groceries and goodies. Ken Griffey Jr. (above) watches a longball leave the Kingdome.

Denver

When 80,227 enthusiastic fans welcomed the Colorado Rockies on the franchise's first Opening Day at Mile High Stadium on April 9, 1993, it confirmed the belief that Denver was hungry for Major League Baseball. As the only Big League outfit then located in the Mountain Time Zone, the Rockies emerged quickly as a true regional franchise and drew a Big League–record 4,483,350 fans in their inaugural season.

MOUNTAIN TIME

Although the fans took to the Rockies with the zeal of the newly converted, baseball had been popular in the Rocky Mountains going back to 1862, when George Tebeau organized a club called the Denvers that would later play in the Western League. In 1913, Denver's franchise adopted the name the Bears, a team best known for its Triple-A incarnation between 1955–92. With the local organization's Major League ties changing seemingly every few years, former Bears like Tim Raines, Graig Nettles and Terry Francona reached The Show with different clubs around the Majors. The Bears also launched the managing careers of Billy Martin and Felipe Alou.

In 1985, the team became affiliated with the Reds and was dubbed the Denver Zephyrs, after the famous passenger train that runs through the Rocky Mountains. Barry Larkin and Greg Vaughn were among the last stars of the Triple-A Denver franchise before it moved to New Orleans in 1993, in order to make way for the Rockies. The front office of the fledgling Rockies shrewdly assembled a club of big-hitters, tailor-made for Denver's thin air. In 1995, Andres Galarraga, Dante Bichette and Vinny Castilla led the club to the playoffs in just its third season — and the team's very first year playing in Coors Field.

For the rest of the decade the Rockies, led by Larry Walker and Todd Helton, continued to lead the NL in attendance. The team's popularity never waned even when attendance figures weren't breaking records. In 2007, Colorado snapped out of a mid-season malaise and embarked on a historic hot streak, winning 21 of 22 games after

Sept. 15, en route to the club's first NL pennant and World Series appearance.

BREW HA-HA

Outsiders sometimes view Colorado residents as outdoorsy types who are too busy hiking and mountain biking to sit still for a few leisurely hours and take in a ballgame. And while there's definitely no shortage of recreational opportunities, especially in the nearby communities of Boulder, Vail, Aspen and Breckenridge, the citizens of Denver take their sports seriously. Just ask fans of the Denver Broncos, who have perhaps the most loyal regional following of any team in the NFL.

Although the Rockies may no longer lead the National League in attendance — as they did in their first seven seasons — the club's return to

PLANES, TRAINS & AUTOMOBILES

The easiest way to get around Denver is aboard one of the free shuttle buses that run the length of downtown, which is 25 miles from Denver International Airport. Even with gratis buses whisking visitors around the city, those travelers who want to explore the surrounding area should rent a car. During baseball season, however, lucky travelers may be upgraded to SUVs since most of the rental car companies are accustomed to dealing with ski vacationers looking for four-wheel drive transportation in the winter.

"Dinger" (above) was named after dinosaur fossils were found at the ballpark's site. An original member of the Rockies, Andres Galarraga was key to the club's early success.

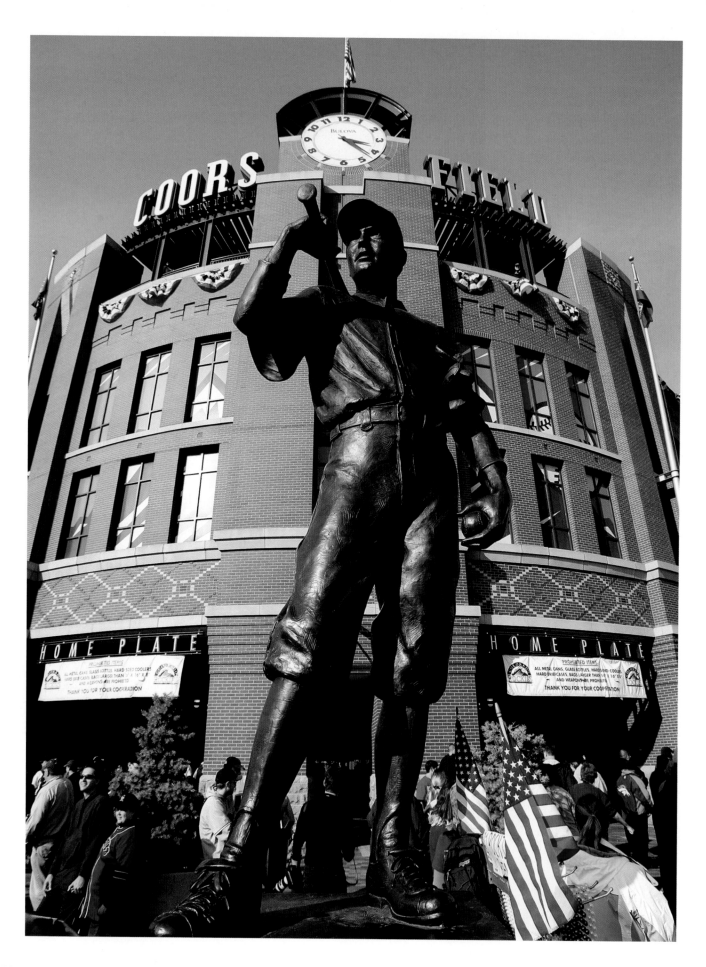

prominence, thanks to emerging stars such as Troy Tulowitzki and Ubaldo Jimenez, has only bolstered the team's local interest.

Even if early April's chilly weather can seem a bit too harsh for baseball, Rockies fans are passionate about their team and come out in droves from Opening Day to whenever the team is in the hunt for a division crown or the Wild Card.

Like many of the expansive back-to-the-future ballparks built over the last 20 years, Coors Field was designed to fit into a city block, making it feel like a true neighborhood ballpark akin to Chicago's Wrigley Field and Brooklyn's former Ebbets Field. That helps give Denver's lower downtown "LoDo" district one of the best old-school baseball atmospheres anywhere, even if the park is just 15 years old.

The Sports Column, located just steps from Coors Field on Blake Street, has been rated among the top sports bars in America by ESPN.com, *Sports Illustrated* and *The Sporting News* and is the spot in LoDo to meet and greet fellow seamheads.

COOR-DIALLY YOURS
Coors Field was the first ballpark built in the post–Camden Yards boom of stadium construction that featured a lower concourse which encircled the field, enabling fans to wander the park without missing a single pitch. Built when the Rockies were setting baseball attendance records at Mile High Stadium, Coors Field can fit 50,445 fans. To help keep everyone close to the action, there's precious little foul territory, which produces plenty of souvenir balls.

Despite its size, Coors is kid friendly, from the jungle gym to the two sections of alcohol-free seating — a welcome touch in a building named

after a beer company. That's one of many fan-friendly aspects of the ballpark, built on 1.4 million square feet of land that once included the city's first railroad depot. It's the only park in the Majors where fans can sit in a designated row of seats painted purple and know they're exactly 5,280 feet — one mile — above sea level. Plus, there's a stunning view of the Front Range of the Rocky Mountains beyond left and center field.

Coors' Sandlot Brewery sits behind the right-field stands and is the site where Blue Moon, a popular Belgian-style white beer, was first brewed. There's no shortage of food to complement all the beverages, including sushi, burritos and just about anything that can be thrown on a grill. Many believe Coors Field also produces some of the game's best pizza. Then there are the infamous Rocky Mountain oysters, which tend to attract the bold "I'll try anything once" crowd. For those who don't know what the oysters are, go ahead and look them up — we'll wait.

MUST-SEE MOUNTAIN SPOTS
Tourists flock to Colorado during the winter to hit the slopes, but baseball fans visiting Denver during the Big League season will find that there is a lot to do even when the chairlifts aren't running. Downtown Denver is home to the Colorado History Museum, Daniels and Fisher Tower (inspired by St. Mark's Cathedral in Venice), the Denver Art Museum and the Denver Children's Museum.

The 16th Street Mall, a pedestrian-only stretch of 12 blocks shaded by oak and locust trees, is a prime people-watching spot with more than 1,000 chairs and benches set aside to take in the scene. The pristine mall area is full of outdoor cafes, historic buildings and shops. Making up the

area itself is a composite of rose and gray granite.

For many out-of-town fans, no trip to Colorado is complete without a tour of the Coors Brewing Company. The brewery can be found in the town of Golden, just 16 miles west of Denver. More than 250,000 people take the free tour each year. If just one libation doesn't suit your palette, there's the New Belgium Brewing Company, which also offers free tours.

Although the Coors Brewing Company ranks impressively as the world's fifth-largest brewer, the branch of the U.S. Mint located in Denver is currently the world's largest producer of coins. More than 10 billion U.S. coins are manufactured there annually. Free tours take guests through the facility, which also houses the nation's second-largest cache of gold.

Along with a deep history of mining settlements, the Rockies are home to many awe-inspiring rock formations, like those found at the Red Rocks Amphitheater. Surrounded by 300-foot-high sandstone cliffs, the picturesque venue is just 18 miles southwest of Denver in the community of Morrison. It has been the site of historic concerts from the likes of U2 and the Grateful Dead, and is also open to visitors on days without any concerts or events.

In the heart of Denver's LoDo district, Coors Field (left) has a neighborhood feel. The Coors Brewery (above) in nearby Golden, Colo., is a must-see spot.

WHAT'S IN A NAME?
In 1976, the NHL launched the Colorado Rockies, but the team later moved to New Jersey, where it enjoyed much success after becoming the Devils. When Major League Baseball announced its return to Colorado in 1991, the lure of the Rocky Mountains was too great, and the owners of the team scooped up the abandoned name.

chapter 4

the upper midwest

MINNEAPOLIS

MILWAUKEE

CHICAGO

DETROIT

TORONTO

Minneapolis

The Minnesota Twins' long-held home-field advantage became a thing of the past when the club moved from the cacophonous Metrodome into open-air Target Field. Despite the area's reputation as having a generally unwelcoming climate, visitors of Minneapolis during baseball season will be delighted to discover that few regions of the country are as wonderful as the "Land of 10,000 Lakes."

A TALE OF TWIN CITIES

The Metrodome was constructed in Minneapolis to shield athletes from the area's cold, often inclement weather. One would think that road teams coming to play against the Twins in October would appreciate the gesture, especially those clubs like the Atlanta Braves, coming from warm climates. Yet it's a safe bet that most Braves players would rather have played Game 7 of the 1991 World Series in a sub-zero blizzard than under the thunderous onslaught of noise constantly reverberating inside the dome. With the championship on the line, Minnesota native Jack Morris edged young Braves ace John Smoltz in an extra-inning pitchers' duel before more than 55,000 fans.

With his bat and unabashed enthusiasm, the stout outfielder Kirby Puckett was an integral part of the '91 championship team and became the most beloved player in franchise history. But he wasn't the first all-time great to play in the Twin Cities.

The Minneapolis Millers appeared in several incarnations beginning in 1884, until becoming an American Association franchise from 1902–60. Through the years, the Millers were affiliated with the New York Giants and twice with the Boston Red Sox, fielding teams with future Hall of Famers Ted Williams, Willie Mays, Carl Yastrzemski, Ray Dandridge, Orlando Cepeda, Monte Irvin and Hoyt Wilhelm.

Across the Mississippi River in nearby St. Paul, the first edition of the St. Paul Saints played from 1884 to 1899, eventually joining the Western League. In 1900, the Western League became the American League, and Saints Owner Charles Comiskey relocated the club to Chicago, where it became the White Sox.

St. Paul again hosted a team called the Saints from 1902–60 that competed in the American Association along with the Millers. These Saints, affiliated with the Chicago White Sox and Brooklyn-turned-L.A. Dodgers, enjoyed a strong rivalry with the Minneapolis Millers.

When Calvin Griffith relocated his Washington Senators to Minnesota, he wanted to attract fans from both St. Paul and Minneapolis, so he settled on "Twins" for the team's nickname. During the club's last 14 seasons in Washington, the Senators had never finished above fifth place in the American League, but the same group of players began to show improvement in Minnesota. The Twins won 89 or more games in five of

Manager Ron Gardenhire's (opposite, right) Twins faced Boston in the first regular-season game at Target Field in April 2010. Minneapolis's many lakes are popular destinations.

their first eight seasons with Tony Oliva, Harmon Killebrew and Rod Carew before winning the first two AL West titles after baseball expanded to divisional play for the 1969 campaign.

From 1971–2001, the Twins reached the playoffs just twice, but won a pair of memorable World Series titles in 1987 and 1991 under Manager Tom Kelly. Since 2002, the Twins, led by skipper Ron Gardenhire, have been regular playoff participants. The club shrewdly manages its payroll to compete with baseball's financial juggernauts and has also produced a great deal of homegrown talent, including catcher Joe Mauer, who hails from St. Paul.

RIGHT ON TARGET

In 2010, the Twins welcomed outdoor Major League ball back to the North

Star State for the first time since 1981. After nearly 30 years of playing in the cavernous Metrodome, Target Field fits just 39,504 with a design that allows a fan seated in the top row in left field to be as close to the action as one in the first row of the Metrodome's upper deck. Instead of building yet another Camden Yards clone of red brick and exposed steel, the Twins used stone and a glass wall exterior, perhaps ushering in another era of design.

The ballpark pays tribute to the Twins' rich history, with each entrance gate numbered after a former player's retired jersey. There's 3 for Harmon Killebrew, 6 for Tony Oliva, 14 for Kent Hrbek, 29 for Rod Carew and 34 for Kirby Puckett.

Located on the western edge of downtown Minneapolis, Target Field provides a festive atmosphere. Every Twins longball at the state-of-the-art park

ignites a multimedia explosion. There are flashing lights and fireworks, and a sign in center field featuring mascots Minnie and Paul over what appears to be a flowing Mississippi River, while "Let's Go Crazy" by music icon and Minnesota native Prince is played.

DOME-FIELD ADVANTAGE

Baseball fans from elsewhere may not know too much about Twins fans beyond the "homer hankies" that gained notoriety during the 1987 World Series, but visiting players have learned about the power of the locals pretty quickly. Playing the Cardinals in the '87 Fall Classic, Twins fans made some of the highest-decibel noise ever recorded during the World Series. With the Twins behind in the Series, 3 games to 2, the fans pumped up the volume, rallying the team to victory in seven games.

Twins fans have always embraced players with personalities that fit the hard-nosed but upbeat way of the city, from Kent Hrbek and Kirby Puckett to Chuck Knoblauch and Justin Morneau. The front office has also brought home native sons such as Jack Morris, Dave Winfield and Paul Molitor. Most recently, they drafted and developed hometown hero Joe Mauer into one of the game's biggest stars. The St. Paul native won three AL batting titles and an MVP Award in his first five full seasons in the Bigs.

MALL-GOPHERS

The Mall of America in suburban Bloomington, Minn., stands on the former site of Metropolitan Stadium, once home to the Twins and the NFL's Vikings. In the mall's amusement park, there's a plaque commemorating the former location of home plate.

A bit further afield, the Minnesota Amateur Baseball Hall of Fame at the St. Cloud Civic Center chronicles the state's long history with the sport, which goes back to at least 1857.

To watch the next wave of talent, check out a game at the University of Minnesota. The Gophers baseball team has produced Hall of Famers like Dave Winfield and Paul Molitor, and also Dan Wilson and Denny Neagle. The St. Paul Saints are one of the most popular clubs in independent league baseball, which isn't affiliated with the Majors.

GREAT BY THE LAKES

Minnesota is known as the "Land of 10,000 Lakes" and Minneapolis's Chain of Lakes — Lake Calhoun, Lake of the Isles, Cedar Lake, Brownie Lake and Lake Harriet — shows that the nickname is no exaggeration. Minnehaha Falls in South Minneapolis is also a popular destination.

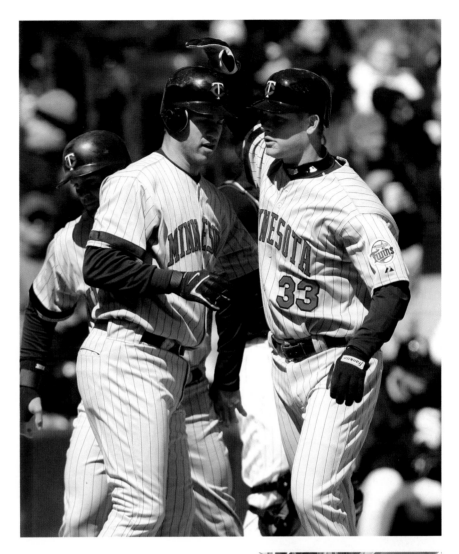

Art buffs love to stroll through the Minneapolis Sculpture Garden, with its tree-lined walkways and collection of public art. The Minneapolis Institute of Arts is also popular, featuring more than 80,000 sculptures, paintings, drawings and photography spanning 4,000 years.

On a clear day, it's possible to see all the way to St. Paul from the observation deck of Foshay Tower.

WHAT'S IN A NAME?
After relocating his Senators from Washington to Minnesota, Owner Calvin Griffith wanted to make sure his new fanbase included people from both of the twin cities of Minneapolis and St. Paul. Eliminating "Twin Cities" and "Twin City Twins" as names, Griffith landed on the Minnesota Twins. The team's first home game was ironically against Washington's new expansion team, once again named the Senators.

Twins fans waved their "homer hankies" at the Metrodome during the 1991 World Series (opposite). Frequent All-Stars Joe Mauer and Justin Morneau (top, left to right) keep the excitement alive for Twins fans. The Mall of America in Bloomington has shopping and rides.

Milwaukee

Known as the "City of Festivals," Milwaukee welcomes visitors with open arms and a raised glass. Whether it's tailgating before a ballgame at Miller Park or a concert at the annual Summerfest, there's always something fun happening. A vibrant ethnic mix has given the city a European feel in the heart of Wisconsin, and the Brewers have embraced their home town's cuisine with their famous sausage races.

BREW CITY

Baseball teams in Milwaukee have been playing under the name Brewers since the 1870s. When the American League's Milwaukee Brewers moved to St. Louis and became the Browns in 1902, the Minor League American Association had a new Brewers franchise ready for that season. That Brewers incarnation lasted until 1952, winning several league titles and captivating a young fan in future-Commissioner of Baseball, Bud Selig, along the way. In 1941, Bill Veeck and former Cubs star Charlie Grimm bought the team. Veeck staged numerous stunts and promotions for the upstart club, including the use of live animals and scheduling morning games for nightshift workers during wartime. During Veeck's five years at the helm, the team won three AA pennants.

In 1953, Milwaukee embraced its first Major League club in 52 years when the Braves arrived from Boston to play in the newly constructed County Stadium. Locals were certainly excited, as 1.8 million fans came out to the ballpark to see the team during its inaugural season, setting a National League record. Thanks to the tremendous fan support and the slugging prowess of Hank Aaron and Eddie Mathews, the Braves reached the World Series in 1957 and '58, defeating the Yankees in '57. The team never posted a losing season in its 13 years in Milwaukee before disappointing locals by moving to Atlanta after the 1965 campaign.

Selig worked tirelessly to bring Major League Baseball back to Milwaukee, engineering the relocation of the expansion Seattle Pilots after their inaugural 1969 season. Due in part to the sudden arrival of the ballclub, the first-ever Major League Brewers kept the Pilots' original colors of blue and gold.

Led by future Hall of Famers Rollie Fingers, Robin Yount and Paul Molitor, the Brewers were a powerhouse in the late 1970s and early 1980s, winning the AL pennant in 1982. With potent bats up and down the lineup and fiery Manager Harvey Kuenn calling the shots, the club became known as "Harvey's Wallbangers."

In part because of the success of the Braves, Selig viewed Milwaukee as more of a National League market,

PLANES, TRAINS & AUTOMOBILES

Miller Park, like County Stadium before it, is famous for its pregame tailgating. So perhaps it's appropriate to drive to the ballgame. For those looking to burn a few calories before filling up on bratwurst and beer, the Hank Aaron Trail, a 7-mile walking and cycling trail that runs past the park, is an option for fans staying nearby.

Brewers fans keep the tailgating tradition alive before games at Miller Park.

prompting the move to the Senior Circuit in 1998 when baseball again expanded. Despite the proximity to Chicago, the Brewers never had a fierce rivalry with the AL's White Sox, and are just beginning to develop an enmity with the Cubs.

Playing in the club's new home, Miller Park, young sluggers Ryan Braun and Prince Fielder again put the Brew Crew atop the longball leaderboards.

PARTY ON
While on a tour of Big League ballparks for ESPN.com, writer Jim Caple remarked, "baseball never smells so good as it does in the Milwaukee parking lot."

Wisconsin is famous for its tailgating, as fans of the Green Bay Packers and Wisconsin Badgers can attest, and the Brewers have by far the best tailgate scene in baseball. With sprawling parking lots full of early arrivals grilling bratwursts, sausages and hot dogs, it's no wonder some fans don't enter Miller Park until at least the third inning.

Perhaps it's the food or the fact that the Braves were so successful in Milwaukee, but Brew City fans have a positive outlook on the game. They

never succumbed to apathy or melancholy, even when the Brewers got off to a slow start in their early years in the American League.

BERNIE'S PLACE
Veeck launched his career as baseball's most famous promoter as owner of the Milwaukee Brewers of the American Association from 1941–45. Six decades later, the Brewers still have some of the best game-day promotions, including the world-famous Klement Sausage Race in the middle of the sixth inning. Mascot Bernie Brewer also slides down a yellow slide into the "splash zone"— sending water shooting into the air out in left field — following every Brewers home run.

The Associated Bank Kids Zone, located on the field level near the right-field corner, is an entertainment area that includes a batting cage, pitching cage, another Bernie Brewer slide and clubhouse, as well as an interactive game with replicas of the Klement's racing sausage mascots.

Fans who haven't eaten their fill during the pregame tailgating — or who had their appetite whetted by the

WHAT'S IN A NAME?
Milwaukee has always taken pride in its pitchers — of beer, at least. With such a rich community of breweries, it was a no-brainer for the "Beer Capital of the World" to factor them into the naming of its baseball team. The toast of the town in Milwaukee naturally became the Brewers.

famous race — can enjoy Italian or Polish sausages, chorizo, bratwurst or hot dogs, all generously covered with the Brewers' legendary "secret sauce." Gorman Thomas, the beloved Brewers outfielder of the 1980s, appears during weekend games at the "Gorman's Corner" concession stand.

HOME AWAY FROM HOME

At Lakefront Brewery, fans not only enjoy some of the city's top beers but they can also pay homage to Bernie Brewer. Lakefront President Russ Klisch purchased Bernie's original chalet and slide after the team left County Stadium and moved both to his brewery. Many members of the Brewers franchise have even autographed Bernie's old home. Although most of County Stadium has become parking for Miller Park, the site of the old infield was converted into a Little League park called Helfaer Field.

THE 'B's ARE JUST THE BEGINNING

Fans visiting Milwaukee tend to focus on the "B's" — baseball, beer, bratwurst

The Harley-Davidson Museum (far left). Ryan Braun (left, center) high-fives team-mates after a homer. Commissioner of Baseball and area-native Bud Selig.

and bikes. Miller Park certainly provides the first three, and the latter can be found at the nearby Harley-Davidson Museum, which has a vast display of vintage motorcycles, as well as plenty of other Americana to peruse. Even non-bikers love the museum's many interesting exhibits.

Beer and architecture buffs alike enjoy the Pabst Mansion, which is built in Flemish Renaissance style to honor Captain Frederick Pabst, founder of Pabst Brewing Company. Miller Brewing Company, a subsidiary of MillerCoors (one of the world's largest brewers, which also owns Pabst) offers free tours.

Although it's known for those "B's," Milwaukee is an underrated destination for art and culture. The Milwaukee Art Museum features the works of Pablo Picasso, Georgia O'Keeffe and Andy Warhol. For the kids, visit the Milwaukee County Zoo and the interactive Betty Brinn Children's Museum.

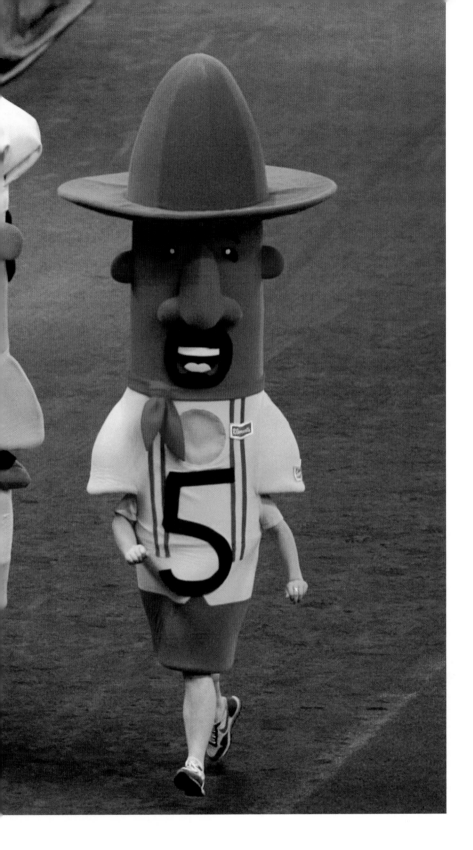

During the warmer summer months, visitors can attend one of the city's many ethnic festivals, stroll the downtown Riverwalk or take in the sites of the Historic Third Ward. There are also countless recreational opportunities available for outdoorsy types on Lake Michigan.

Summerfest, held annually since 1968 on the 75-acre Henry Maier Festival Grounds, is the world's largest music festival. The event runs from late June through early July and features 11 stages and more than 700 performers representing rock, blues, R&B, reggae and other genres.

The Klement's Sausage Race, inspired by the area's must-try bratwurst and other sausages, takes place at Miller Park during the sixth inning.

Chicago

Heartbreak has been served up to Chicago hardball fans almost as often as the city's deep-dish pizza during the more than 100 years of Big League baseball in the Windy City. Perhaps it's the blustery winters and the silent autumns that have made fans on both sides of town so resilient. With a gameday atmosphere that's hard to beat, Chicago is a must-see spot on any baseball itinerary.

LONG TIME COMING

When burly Chicago White Sox closer Bobby Jenks induced a weak groundout from Houston Astros pinch-hitter Orlando Palmeiro for the final out in Game 4 of the 2005 World Series, there was a feeling of jubilation in the Windy City more than 80 years in the making. Heading into the '05 Fall Classic, the Sox hadn't claimed a world title since 1917, and the crosstown Cubs hadn't tasted success since 1908. Thanks to an unflappable pitching staff and the bat of veteran slugger Jermaine Dye, the Sox ripped through the postseason and claimed the title for Chicago.

Although the lack of championship hardware for most of the 20th century could lead one to forget the club's historic roots, professional baseball came to Chicago shortly after the founding of the game's first openly professional team. The Cincinnati Red Stockings first paid players in 1869, and the Chicago White Stockings debuted in 1870. The Chicago club then joined the fledgling National League six years later.

The team competed as the Colts and the Orphans before becoming the Cubs in 1903. Behind the pitching of Mordecai "Three Finger" Brown and the famed double-play combination of Joe Tinker, Johnny Evers and Frank Chance, the Cubs won four NL pennants between 1906 and '10, taking the World Series crown in both 1907 and '08.

When the American League debuted in 1900, it unearthed the White Stockings moniker for a charter franchise in Chicago. Headline writers referred to the team as the "Sox," and the name eventually stuck. The Sox defeated the crosstown Cubs to win the World Series in 1906 and topped the New York Giants in 1917. They were favored over the Reds in the 1919 Fall Classic, but then lost in the infamous Black Sox Scandal, as members of the team conspired with gamblers.

Through the years, Chicago baseball has splintered into two distinct camps. The North Siders pull for the Cubs while the South Side roots for the Sox. But one family has

PLANES, TRAINS & AUTOMOBILES

When it comes to getting around Chicago, one immediately thinks of the El — and for good reason. The elevated train, which has stops near both ballparks, is definitely the simplest way to traverse the city. Although there's plenty of parking at U.S. Cellular Field, there is absolutely none at Wrigley Field or many places around town. Either way, Chicago is a city where it's best to forego the rental car and take mass transit. Otherwise, taxis are another convenient option.

Chicago's beautiful skyline may be the one thing on which Cubs and White Sox fans agree.

managed to work both sides of town. The Veeck family played an all-around key role in Chicago baseball. William Veeck, a former sportswriter, served as Cubs President from 1919 until his death in 1933. His son, Bill, planted the famous ivy that covers the Wrigley Field walls in 1937. The younger Veeck later owned the Cleveland Indians and St. Louis Browns before two stints as owner of the White Sox. As the Sox owner, Veeck installed the much-copied "exploding scoreboard" at Comiskey Park and was the first to put players' names on the backs of uniforms.

THE IVY LEAGUE

The term "lovable loser" is apropos for the Cubs franchise since it has always been hip to be a Cubs fan, no matter how many years — or decades — have passed since the club's last World Series triumph. In the 1980s, Illinois native and famous comedian/actor Bill Murray and fictional high schooler Ferris Bueller did their part to make being a Chicago Cubs fan fashionable.

One of the last bastions of regular daytime baseball, raucous Wrigley Field can sometimes seem more like a beer garden than a baseball stadium. The atmosphere was inspired in part by the gregarious former broadcaster Harry Caray, whose announcing style was heavily influenced by his unabashed fandom. He would lead fans in a sing-along rendition of "Take Me Out to the Ballgame" during the seventh-inning stretch.

Wrigley Field has attracted a boisterous crowd that's just as concerned with the party as it is with the game. That mentality prompted former Cubs Manager Lee Elia's legendary post-game tirade in 1983. "Eighty-five percent of the world is working," he ranted. "The other 15 percent come out here."

There are also many popular bars around Wrigley Field to enjoy pregame and post-game frivolity, including The Cubby Bear, Sluggers and Murphy's Bleachers. Sluggers even offers an indoor batting cage for patrons.

For all their rowdy behavior, Cubs fans are a knowledgeable and devoted bunch, embracing longtime

players such as Ernie Banks, Ron Santo, Mark Grace and Sammy Sosa. Bill Veeck spent his final years amid the bleacher bums.

With the White Sox winning the World Series in 2005 and the Red Sox finally breaking their own streak of futility, Cubs fans have the long-suffering label all to themselves. It's as much a part of the fan culture as Old Style beer, ivy and Caray's off-key singing.

THE FRIENDLY CONFINES

Wrigley Field can seem crowded to some, especially visiting outfielders, but few ballparks have inspired such a great connection between a city, its team and its fans.

As one of baseball's last original temples, and the only remaining Federal League park, Wrigley Field is a piece of history. The convivial atmosphere more than makes up for the lack of modern

amenities and sideshow diversions that characterize today's stadiums. Cubs fans learned long ago to entertain themselves, turning Wrigley into baseball's biggest house party.

Wrigley Field's ivy-covered wall (opposite) is as beloved as late voice Harry Caray (bottom). Caray and Hack Wilson are two of many icons honored at Wrigley.

Since Wrigley has some of baseball's best traditions, there's no need for any high-tech gimmicks. Some fans, instead of watching batting practice, congregate along Waveland Avenue with the ballhawks and compete for home run balls that leave the park altogether. Another tradition, which exists elsewhere but seems particularly well-suited to Wrigley, is the practice of throwing back home run balls hit by opponents. This may strike some souvenir-happy fans as sacrilege, but it still seems appropriate at Wrigley.

Since the passing of the club's longtime announcer Harry Caray in 1998, a number of celebs from Murray to John Cusack to Mr. T have lined up for the chance to appear during the seventh-inning stretch and lead the fans in the singing of "Take Me Out to the Ballgame" — a tradition Caray brought with him when he moved to Wrigley from Comiskey Park.

SOUTH SIDERS

Over the years, White Sox fans have learned to accept their favorite club's status as the oft-overlooked younger sibling to the more prominent Chicago team — the Cubs. Happy to let the Cubs have the tourists and the media crush, White Sox fans embrace the team's blue-collar status.

Longtime Sox Owner Jerry Reinsdorf is the polar opposite of his predecessor, the madcap promoter Bill Veeck, who ran the team from 1959–61 and then again from 1975–81. Nevertheless, the

park that opened under Reinsdorf's watch in 1991, called U.S. Cellular Field, retained a version of Veeck's "exploding" scoreboard, and the White Sox marketing department pays tribute to Veeck's hijinks with a variety of creative promotions.

As if the tough reputation of the South Side wasn't strong enough, Sox fans seem to take their cue from imposing former slugger Frank Thomas, dubbed the "Big Hurt," and feisty shortstop-turned-skipper Ozzie Guillen. With a 2005 World Series title and a fan in the White House, White Sox supporters are content that their club has overshadowed the Cubs on the field, if not in the national consciousness. President Barack Obama has proudly proclaimed his allegiance to the club, wearing a White Sox jacket when he took the field

for the ceremonial first pitch at the 2009 All-Star Game in St. Louis.

QUITE ALL WHITE

Young White Sox fans don't make a trip to U.S. Cellular Field just to watch the Big Leaguers. Many can't wait to head over to the 15,000-square-foot Pontiac Fundamentals area that features a youth-sized Wiffle ball diamond, batting and pitching cages, batting "swing" boxes and areas for baserunning and skills instruction.

The Sox opened U.S. Cellular Field in 1991, the year before Baltimore's Oriole Park at Camden Yards ushered in the era of retro ballparks. "New Comiskey," as it was known at the time, featured a design that, from the outside, made it look like the sort of multipurpose cookie-cutter ballpark that had been

WHAT'S IN A NAME?
In 1900, Owner Charles Comiskey joined the American League with a Chicago team. The club took its name "White Stockings" from an old National League team, but *Chicago Tribune* sportswriters Carl Green and Irving Sanborn, struggling to squeeze "Stockings" into headline space, creatively found a solution with White Sox.

The Cell has lots of options (near right).
Barack Obama (opposite) displayed Sox
pride even before becoming president.

in vogue in the 1970s and '80s. Since 2001, though, the ballpark has undergone several renovations that have made it look and feel more like today's ironically "retro" ballparks.

The park features two blue seats, one located behind the left-field fence and the other behind the right-field fence, which are marked to commemorate a pair of home runs hit by Paul Konerko and Scott Podsednik during Game 2 of the 2005 World Series.

GONE BUT NOT FORGOTTEN

With two teams having called Chicago home for more than a century, Illinois became the final resting place for Hall of Famers including Cap Anson, Charles Comiskey, Red Faber, William Harridge, Fred Lindstrom and Ray Schalk. No two are interred in the same cemetery, so paying your respects will take some traversing of the state.

SECOND TO NONE

Many Chicago baseball visitors are content to spend their time sampling the many bars and restaurants in "Wrigleyville" — the neighborhood surrounding the Cubs' Wrigley Field and sprawling out from North Clark and West Addison streets. But those fans are missing out on all the wonderful attractions that Chicago has to offer.

The Art Institute of Chicago is home to one of the world's largest collections of contemporary and modern art. Chicago also has two of the nation's best zoos. Lincoln Park Zoo, on the North Side, is free and open every day of the year. Brookfield Zoo, located just west of Chicago, is situated on 216 acres of well-manicured grounds and features more than 2,000 animals. And the Navy Pier is a one-stop all-inclusive entertainment destination located on

Lake Michigan that features multiple amusement park rides, restaurants and shops. Navy Pier also is home to the Chicago Shakespeare Theater, an IMAX theater and the Smith Museum of Stained Glass windows. The Pier has two performance stages, and top local bands host free shows for the public every May through October.

No trip to the Windy City is complete without climbing to the 103rd-floor skydeck of the Willis Tower, formerly known as the Sears Tower and currently the world's fifth-largest building, for a view from more than 1,350 feet high.

The Cubs squared off against the White Sox in the 1906 World Series (left), which the South Siders won, 4 games to 2. The Chicago Theatre marquee is a city landmark.

Detroit

Just in case being the nerve center of the American auto industry and the home of the fabled Motown sound wasn't enough, Detroit Tigers players from Ty Cobb to Kirk Gibson have made sure that the tough-as-nails Motor City is synonymous with baseball, too. The fact that it's one of a handful of cities represented by all four major sports ensures a population of passionate and well-versed fans.

ROCK CITY

In the years following the Civil War, baseball became an increasingly popular pastime around the country. In Detroit, it became more of a civic duty. The Detroit Wolverines entered the National League in 1881 at the behest of Mayor William G. Thompson. The city's first Major League team brought home the pennant to the then-motorless city in 1887. The Wolverines would last just one more season in the NL, but top-flight baseball would re-emerge in Detroit when the Tigers debuted in 1894 as a member of the Western League, a forerunner to the American League.

In 1905, Ty Cobb made his Detroit debut as an 18-year-old and went on to be the star of three consecutive AL pennant winners from 1907–09. Ruthless and fearless, Cobb played with a mean streak and was arguably the greatest player of his era.

The team's home at the corner of Michigan Avenue and Trumbull Street — Bennett Park — was demolished in 1911, and the Tigers built a new fireproof steel and concrete structure on the same site. Originally known as Navin Field when it opened in 1912, the ballpark was dubbed Briggs Stadium for years before simply being known as Tiger Stadium from 1961 until its closing in 1999.

Playing in Tiger Stadium, the club won four World Series titles, one of them in 1935, thanks to a record-setting infield featuring Hank Greenberg and Charlie Gehringer. The Tigers won another in 1945, but it was the 1968 season that would go down as one of the most memorable in franchise history. Riding the one-two punch of pitchers Denny McLain, who went 31-6, and Mickey Lolich, who came up huge in the Fall Classic, the Tigers defeated the Cardinals in seven games in the '68 Series.

Mark "The Bird" Fidrych became a national cult hero in 1976 with his zany mound antics, winning 19 games and packing Tiger Stadium to the rafters. Eight years later, in 1984, the Tigers and Manager Sparky Anderson built upon an unbelievable 35-5 start to win their fourth World Series, with help from "Mr. Clutch," Kirk Gibson, in his breakout season. Gibson hit 27 home runs, swiped 29 bases and knocked in 91 runs while raking at a .282 clip.

From 1989–2005, the Tigers posted just two winning seasons, but fans kept their faith, especially after moving to Comerica Park. In 2006, under new Manager Jim Leyland, the Tigers won 95

games and reached the World Series before losing to St. Louis in five games.

SPORTING THEIR STRIPES

With Ernie Harwell — one of the most beloved voices in baseball history — as the patriarch, and Tiger Stadium and Comerica Park among its beloved homes, it's no wonder that the Tigers' fanbase has become a tight-knit family.

The Tigers are one of few teams, along with the Yankees and Red Sox, who inspire local citizens to wear their caps to show provincial pride, even if they don't follow baseball. This was even true long before Detroit native Tom Selleck made Tigers lids fashionable on the 1980s television show *Magnum P.I.*

The team has a classic logo and uniform, along with a history of iconic

A carousel at Comerica Park (above) features tigers instead of horses, and is always a source of fun for young fans. Ty Cobb (right), known for his aggressive play and attitude, debuted with the Tigers in 1905 and spent 22 seasons with the team.

The Tigers pay tribute to their namesake all over Comerica Park, which features claw marks and giant sculptures (top). Kirk Gibson (above, center) celebrates his momentous eighth-inning home run in the 1984 World Series. (Opposite, left to right) Hank Greenberg, Goose Goslin, Charlie Gehringer and Pete Fox were key members of the club in the 1930s.

players and a knack for hiring high-profile, outspoken managers who fit the blue-collar city. That elite group includes Jim Leyland, Ralph Houk, Billy Martin and Sparky Anderson.

In recent years it has not been difficult to upstage the Detroit Lions of the NFL for the attention of the citizenry. But even though the NBA's Pistons and NHL's Red Wings have been far more successful over the last 25 years, it's the Tigers who seem to represent the pulse of Detroit. Thanks to more than a century of existence, the Tigers are inherently intertwined with the city's history.

COME TOGETHER

Tiger Stadium, one of baseball's beloved classic ballparks, was a tough act for Comerica Park to follow. Somehow, though, it has managed to succeed.

No team better integrates its name into its ballpark's architecture: Giant tiger statues guard the main entrance; there are stone tiger heads mounted on the exterior walls, each holding a lighted baseball in its mouth; and there are Tiger claw marks down the walls.

With fireworks and constant music, the so-called "experience" can seem overdone at some new Major League ballparks, but at Comerica it creates an old-time carnival atmosphere. The merry-go-round in the food court fittingly features tigers instead of horses and the 50-foot Fly Ball Ferris Wheel located in the Brushfire Grill has cars shaped like giant baseballs. A "liquid fireworks" display from the fountain in the center-field wall celebrates every single Tigers home run. Given the amusement park feeling, it's a definite must to have a delicious Coney dog smothered in chili, onions and cheese, or at least pay a visit to Beer Hall, a 70-foot bar that offers a variety of local and international brews.

As for history, the Tigers brought it from the corner of Michigan and Trumbull. There are detailed exhibits honoring each decade of the Tigers' club history in the concourses, lest anyone forget about the dominance of the 1968 and '84 teams. Behind center field, there are 13-foot statues of the team's six most revered former

players — Ty Cobb, Charlie Gehringer, Hank Greenberg, Willie Horton, Al Kaline and Hal Newhouser.

FINDING NEMO
Although the team moved out of Tiger Stadium in 1999, fans still visit Nemo's Bar and Grill at 1384 Michigan Avenue on game days. There's still plenty of Tigers memorabilia to make fans feel at home, and Nemo's offers shuttle buses to and from Comerica Park. Aside from Nemo's, though, there's not much to see at the corner of Michigan and Trumbull. After nearly a decade of proposals to save part of Tiger Stadium, demolition was completed on Sept. 21, 2009.

If Nemo's is a bit daunting, the Old Shillelagh is a downtown Irish pub that, like its counterpart, offers shuttle service both to and from Tigers games.

Big fans also have the option to take a 60-mile road trip from Detroit to Toledo, Ohio, to watch the Toledo Mud Hens, a Triple-A affiliate of the Tigers in the International League.

On September Saturdays, Ann Arbor, Mich., hosts America's largest college football crowd at Michigan Stadium, which seats 107,501 fans.

PLANES, TRAINS & AUTOMOBILES
With most visitors to Detroit opting for hotels outside of the downtown area, rental cars are often the best way to get to the stadium, where parking is ample. Traveling into downtown in the evening is no longer the safety concern it once was, with numerous restaurants and bars springing up within a short walk of Comerica Park since its opening. The Detroit People Mover train is also an inexpensive way to get around the city and see many of the sights.

MOTOR AROUND

Considering the fact that Detroit is known as the Motor City, no trip would be complete without a journey to nearby Dearborn to explore the Henry Ford Museum. For more unique local history, another must-see spot is the Motown Historical Museum — a great place to reminisce about performers who came out of Detroit during the 1960s and '70s, including legendary hitmakers such as Marvin Gaye, Diana Ross and Smokey Robinson.

For an active tour of the city, take a stroll along the beautiful Detroit Riverfront, splash in the fountains (weather permitting) or bike alongside a docked freighter. If you didn't get enough of the Comerica merry-go-round, there's a carousel at the Riverfront, too.

If sightseeing works up your appetite, then head to nearby Greektown for some authentic cuisine like gyros or souvlaki. The restaurants and bars have so many delectables that you'll swear you're in Mykonos. Plus, there's also the popular Greektown Casino. If you're looking for even more diversity in culinary choices, the Eastern Market is sprawling with more than 150 farmers and vendors from Michigan, Ohio and Canada, who set up on Saturdays.

Joe Louis Arena is also nearby, and since the NHL's Detroit Red Wings are usually in the playoffs in late spring, it's possible to do a day-night, baseball-hockey doubleheader. In the fall, fans can also piggyback a visit to see the National Football League's Detroit Lions at Ford Field, which is adjacent to Comerica Park.

WHAT'S IN A NAME?

Once called the Wolverines after Michigan's fierce state animal, the *Detroit Free Press* ran the moniker Tigers in an 1895 headline and it caught on. Six years later, Detroit skipper George Stallings allegedly took credit for the name, claiming inspiration from the team's Tiger-like stocking stripes.

Detroit's Motown Museum celebrates iconic performers of the Sixties.

Toronto

Although it's certainly easy to associate Canada with hockey above all else — after all, the Hockey Hall of Fame can be found here — the city of Toronto has established itself as a bona fide Major League hotspot. An incredibly clean and modern metropolis often compared to New York, there's a ton of attractions and character in Toronto. And of course, there's the only baseball franchise in the country.

THE GREAT BLUE NORTH

In the late 1980s and the early 1990s, the largest city in Canada was staking a claim as the capital of America's pastime. The Blue Jays led the AL in attendance from 1989–94, drawing more than 4 million fans in three seasons and winning back-to-back World Series titles under skipper Cito Gaston in 1992 and '93. The 1993 Fall Classic ended on Joe Carter's dramatic home run off Philadelphia's Mitch Williams in Game 6 at SkyDome. As Carter hopped and screamed his way around the bases, there was no doubting Toronto's status as a preeminent Big League city.

Before the Blue Jays arrived as an American League expansion franchise for the 1977 season, Toronto was home to a Minor League team — naturally named the Maple Leafs — that played in the International League from 1912–1967. In 1951, Jack Kent Cooke launched his sports ownership career by purchasing the Maple Leafs and introducing ballpark promotions and giveaways.

Under Cooke, the Leafs even became affiliated with Bill Veeck's St. Louis Browns for the 1951 and '52 seasons. Later, as a Red Sox affiliate managed by Dick Williams in the mid-1960s, the team won back-to-back Governor's Cup titles in the International League. Despite such success, the Maple Leafs struggled financially, were sold and then moved to Louisville, Ky., following the 1967 season. A decade later, Major League Baseball arrived with the Blue Jays, who joined the American League East.

Pat Gillick, the team's assistant general manager, succeeded Peter Bavasi as GM in 1978 and built a farm system that would provide a pipeline of talent throughout his tenure. Gillick's players would just be coming of age as the Jays moved from Exhibition Stadium to the state-of-the-art SkyDome in 1989. With a beautiful new park and a team on the rise, the Jays were on the path to greatness.

FLYING HIGH

When SkyDome — renamed the Rogers Centre in 2005 — opened in 1989, Blue Jays fans took pride in filling up the state-of-the-art building that outshined older venues like Yankee Stadium and Fenway Park. Although Canadians are often hockey fans first and foremost, the Blue Jays led the American League in attendance in the early 1990s as the team captured consecutive World Series titles in '92 and '93. Despite finishing behind the Red Sox and Yankees for most of the 2000s, loyal Jays fans still came out to support their team, and watch Cy Young Award–winner Roy Halladay dominate on the mound.

When winter subsides, Canadian snowbirds and transplants flock to Dunedin (Fla.) Stadium, where the Jays are the only MLB team still playing at their original Spring Training site. Back up north, Jays fans have the most unique seventh-inning stretch in baseball: a fist-pumping, stretching rendition of "Okay Blue Jays" — the team's anthem — that is equal parts group fitness routine *and* battle cry.

THE SKY'S THE LIMIT

When SkyDome opened with its retractable roof, a luxury hotel located just beyond center field and a multi-storied McDonald's restaurant, it seemed like George Jetson himself had been involved with the design. SkyDome, which also hosts the Toronto Argonauts of the Canadian Football League, is impeccable, and offers a unique and exciting fan experience without the bells and whistles of its Major League Baseball successors.

With its ample seating, overnight accommodations and year-round availability, the stadium complex seemed ideal for major concert acts and has hosted a "who's who" of the music world in its first two decades, from artists such as Metallica and Madonna to The Rolling Stones and Paul McCartney and even more contemporary pop stars, such as Avril Lavigne and the Jonas Brothers. Hotel guests can watch the game without leaving their rooms, and some Jays players, such as Roberto Alomar,

PLANES, TRAINS & AUTOMOBILES

Like most bustling cities, Toronto is best seen without a car. It's a great walking city, and there's subway and streetcar service to Rogers Centre. Neighborhoods tend to have a distinct character and even unique architecture, so a walk of just a few blocks can transport travelers seemingly to another city. Just be sure to bring your passport.

The CN Tower (opposite) can be seen from Rogers Centre. The Eaton Centre (top) offers multiple levels of shopping. A fan cheers on the Blue Jays.

have even lived there during their time with the Blue Jays.

Even with the McDonalds long gone, Rogers Centre doesn't lack food options. The Muddy York Market features items — from house-smoked pork to chicken satay and kung pao wraps — as diverse as the neighborhoods that make up Toronto itself. A very popular item among hungry fans is the Buffalo wings bucket at Quaker Steak and Lube in Section 134, the first outlet of the Midwestern restaurant chain in Canada.

INTERNATIONAL PASTIME

The Canadian Baseball Hall of Fame and Museum was relocated from Toronto, 100 miles west, to the city of St. Marys in 1994. But it's worth a trip if you're in the region, as the museum features hundreds of artifacts from Canada's two Major League franchises, the Blue Jays and the late Montreal Expos. There's a collection of memorabilia from Ontario native Ferguson Jenkins, along with a tribute to the early Canadian Minor League teams that featured legends including Jackie Robinson and Tommy Lasorda. Sports fans visiting during the spring are able to catch one of the NHL's original six franchises — the Toronto Maple Leafs — in action.

OH, CANADA

The CN Tower, which is located adjacent to Rogers Centre, is downtown Toronto's most recognizable landmark. Measuring in at 1,815 feet, it held the

title of tallest freestanding structure in the world for more than three decades, until the Burj Khalifa in Dubai surpassed it in 2007. Visitors can travel in a glass elevator to the 1,122-foot high glass-floored outdoor observation deck for an awe-inspiring view of the entire city. The tower also houses a top-floor restaurant.

At just four levels, the Eaton Centre is a less imposing stop on the itinerary, but may be the best place to grab all of your souvenirs. It's a bright, airy shopping mall in the heart of Toronto's downtown area that's home to more than 250 stores. The glass-domed building isn't just a place to spend

your cash — it holds architectural interest as well. Its signature feature is a huge mobile of a flock of Canadian geese, entitled "Flight Stop."

Film buffs should consider visiting during the Toronto International Film Festival, which conveniently takes place during baseball season. It was founded in 1976 and has become one of the most important North American film events, rivaling the famed Cannes Film Festival in France. That's because the Toronto festival, which always begins the Thursday after Labor Day and lasts for 10 days, enables filmmakers to showcase late-year releases and kick off the Oscar race.

Known as SkyDome until 2005 when it was renamed Rogers Centre, Toronto's home field has seen some great baseball, including the emergence of talented left-hander Ricky Romero (above, right), as well as Joe Carter's 1993 World Series walk-off home run (opposite).

chapter 5

the northeast

BOSTON

NEW YORK

PHILADELPHIA

BALTIMORE

WASHINGTON, DC

Boston

Broadcaster Ernie Harwell once said that baseball is "a sport, business — and sometimes even religion." In few places does that quote ring truer than in Boston, where baseball is more than a religion — it's an obsession. With the Celtics, Bruins and Patriots, Boston has an epic sporting pedigree. And yet, no matter how successful those teams are, no franchise is more beloved than the Red Sox.

HUB HARDBALL

Boston's baseball roots run deeper than just the Red Sox. After the Cincinnati Red Stockings of the National Association of Base Ball Players folded in 1870, their manager, Harry Wright, moved to Boston and fielded a team in the new National Association. In 1876, the club joined the National League. The Red Stockings name returned to Cincinnati, while Boston played under a multitude of monikers, including the Red Caps and Doves before becoming the Boston Braves in 1912.

The upstart American League, meanwhile, put together a Boston team in 1901. Originally dubbed the Americans, the club became known as the Red Sox in 1908. The Red Sox moved into Fenway Park in 1912, while the Braves opened Braves Field in 1915. Thanks to the larger capacity of Braves Field, the Sox played home games there during the 1915 and '16 Fall Classics, winning both times. Those triumphs were part of a seven-year stretch that included four Series titles, the last three of which featured Babe Ruth.

After selling Ruth to the Yankees before the 1920 season, the Sox floundered, not capturing another pennant until 1946. The Braves were hapless as well, winning just one flag during that time, in 1948, before departing for Milwaukee after the '52 campaign.

The Red Sox spent the rest of the 20th century providing mostly heartache to their fans. Even successes were tinged with longing. Ted Williams was the finest hitter ever but never won a World Series. Carl Yastrzemski won the Triple Crown during the 1967 "Impossible Dream" season, but the club finished with a World Series loss to St. Louis. And who could forget the gut-wrenching loss to the Mets in the 1986 Fall Classic?

On the verge of another playoff defeat in 2004, the Sox stormed back from a 3-games-to-none deficit against the Yankees in the ALCS before sweeping the Cardinals for their first title since 1918, washing away 86 years of frustration.

PLANES, TRAINS & AUTOMOBILES

Boston is best navigated by foot, especially since its narrow streets are notoriously confusing. For drivers, it's helpful to know that Commonwealth Avenue and Beacon Street run across the heart of the city, from Boston College west of downtown, intersecting a few blocks from Fenway Park, and then hitting Boston Common at the bottom of Beacon Hill. Boston boasts one of the most effective subway systems — the "T" — which was also the nation's first. Geographically, the city is organized around squares, such as Kenmore in Boston and Harvard in nearby Cambridge.

There's always a festive pregame atmosphere on Yawkey Way, outside Fenway Park.

RED SOX NATION

Until 2004, Red Sox fans were united by the suffering brought on by an 86-year championship drought. Fans believed the team was afflicted with "The Curse of the Bambino," which was cast when the team sold Babe Ruth to the rival Yankees in 1920.

Likely due to the legendary curse and history of hard-luck defeats, the Sox boast some of the most literary fans in the country. From ESPN.com columnist Bill Simmons to horror-maven Stephen King, plenty of scribes have drawn inspiration from Fenway Park.

John Henry led a group that bought the Red Sox in 2002 and helped "Red Sox Nation" regain its swagger. As recently as 1998, the Red Sox drew just 2.3 million fans a season, the ninth most in the AL. Tickets to cozy Fenway now rank among the most difficult to get in sports, even with several seating additions including popular seats atop the Green Monster, Fenway's famous left-field wall.

THE MONSTER

Fans looking for retractable roofs and other newfangled bells and whistles found in modern stadiums won't find them at Fenway. That's the charm of the oldest ballpark still in use in the Majors.

In Fenway, which Hall of Famer Tom Seaver once called the "essence of baseball," fans can watch where Smoky Joe Wood pitched and Ted Williams hit. They can see the same Green Monster that Carl Yastrzemski defended so well. They can see where Carlton Fisk coaxed his 12th-inning homer off the foul pole to win Game 6 of the '75 Series.

Although most of Fenway's 37,000-plus seats seem tight by today's standards, there's virtually nowhere to watch the game when not seated. That, too, makes Fenway such a magical throwback; the fans come to watch baseball, not explore an entertainment complex.

Because of Fenway's lack of concourse space, Yawkey Way — the street that runs along the western side of the park — is an outdoor meeting place on game days. It's closed off to traffic three hours before games and offers vendors, music, family entertainment,

bars, restaurants, the team store and the locally televised pregame show. It also features Autograph Alley, where a former player, coach or personality signs free autographs before every home game.

Lansdowne Street, behind the Green Monster, is another spot where fans mingle. Be sure to grab a sausage from one of a dozen private vendors.

BREW'N BALL

The Cask'n Flagon bar on the corner of Brookline Avenue and Lansdowne Street is almost as synonymous with Fenway as the CITGO sign in Kenmore Square that can be seen from home plate. Located in the Green Monster's shadow, The Cask was originally a live-music club but is now a popular sports bar featuring plenty of Sox memorabilia.

Just up "Comm" Ave. from Fenway is Boston University's Nickerson Field. Used

for soccer as well as track and field, it sits on the site of the former Braves Field. Remnants of the park remain, including the right-field pavilion and the original wall in right-center field. The old ticket office is now a University police station.

WHAT'S IN A NAME?
Baseball's first professional team, the NL's Cincinnati Red Stockings, moved to Boston in 1871 and soon changed their name. In 1901, a second Boston team sprang up — this time in the AL — calling itself the Red Stockings in homage to the city's first Big League team. Headline writers shortened it to "Red Sox."

A Boston Duck Tour (opposite) is a great way to explore. Carlton Fisk (above) is greeted after his walk-off homer in 1975.

Although the hockey rivalry between BU and Boston College may draw tons of attention in the Hub, BC's baseball team gets to go head-to-head with the Sox during Spring Training each year.

Fans that come to Boston in the fall may try to pull off a double-header with BC football in the afternoon and a Red Sox game at night. And no matter what time of year a visitor gets to the Bay State, the Sports Museum of New England is always a solid detour. Housed in TD Garden — home to the Celtics and Bruins — the museum pays tribute to all of Boston's sports teams.

BEANTOWN SIGHTS

No U.S. city better blends the old and new than Boston, with its Victorian-era architecture, Revolutionary War history, museums and some of the most notable institutions of higher learning.

Boston Harbor, the Charles River and many parks provide breathing space from the city's hustle and bustle. Many visitors head to the water to get acquainted with the city via the "Birth of a Nation" cruise, which highlights the significance of Boston Harbor before and during the Revolution. Another option is to take one of Boston's famous Duck Tours. Jump inside the WWII-style amphibious landing vehicle and see all of the city's sites from both the streets and the Charles.

In the heart of the city, Boston Common is the starting point for the Freedom Trail, a great way to see 16 prominent sights in a 2.5-mile walking tour. It goes through downtown Boston, the North End (Boston's Little Italy) and Charlestown, and ends at the USS Constitution at the Charlestown Navy Yard.

History buffs won't want to miss the Bunker Hill Monument in Charlestown, either. Other attractions include the Paul Revere House in the North End and downtown's Granary Burying Ground, the resting place for Revere, Samuel Adams and John Hancock.

Tops on the to-do list for many visitors is a trip to Harvard Square, the eclectic gateway to Cambridge, adjacent to Harvard University and a well-traveled pathway for Harvard and MIT students. Others stroll up Newbury Street, window shopping at the posh boutiques.

The Bull & Finch Pub, which provided the inspiration and exterior for the bar in the TV series *Cheers*, is a popular spot, although it's more of a tourist trap than a local pub. Others prefer to take the Boston Brewery Tour. The Samuel Adams brewery is located in Jamaica Plain.

The Red Sox celebrate sweeping the Cardinals in the 2004 World Series (above), while the Cask'n Flagon (right) is a popular meeting spot for fans near Fenway.

New York

New York City is the high-wattage media capital of the world and it loves stars and a good story. Drawing people from all over the globe, the Big Apple represents the country's polyglot melting pot heritage better than anywhere else with its eclectic neighborhoods. It has more to offer than one can discover on just a single visit. And with more than a dozen professional teams, it's a mecca for sports fans.

THE BIG APPLE

Much of baseball history runs through New York City, but to hear a native New Yorker tell it, all of baseball history was made in the Big Apple. From a Cy Young no-hitter at Hilltop Park, to Christy Mathewson and Willie Mays turning heads at the Polo Grounds in Washington Heights; to Jackie Robinson's mad dashes around the basepaths at Ebbets Field in Brooklyn, Aaron Boone's pennant-clinching homer in the House that Ruth Built in the Bronx, and that ball that got by Bill Buckner at Shea Stadium in Queens. Gotham has provided countless baseball memories and been home to some of the most sacred cathedrals in baseball.

Many baseball fans consider the 1950s the Golden Age of baseball, and there is perhaps no era that was more dominated by the "City That Never Sleeps." With three future Hall of Famers patrolling center field in New York — Mickey Mantle for the Yankees, Willie Mays for the Giants and Duke Snider in Brooklyn — at least one New York team played in every World Series with the exception of 1959, when the recently relocated *Los Angeles* Dodgers defeated the Chicago White Sox.

Despite the greatness of Willie, Mickey and the Duke, perhaps no ballplayer looms larger in the American psyche than the Yankees' Babe Ruth. When the Boston Red Sox sold a 24-year-old Ruth to the Yanks prior to the 1920 season, baseball history was changed forever. The Bronx Bombers won their first four World Series championships with Ruth, establishing a multi-decade dynasty that ran all the way through Derek Jeter and Mariano Rivera.

Some of the most storied teams in history — the "Miracle Mets," "Dem Bums" in Brooklyn and the "Murderers' Row" Yankees of Ruth and Lou Gehrig — have been cheered for by New Yorkers. Hustle and relentless effort elevates players to heroic status in this town, and talent and a good personality can make a player a legend.

YA GOTTA BELIEVE

Since joining the Major Leagues as an expansion club in 1962, the Mets have always attracted an eclectic fan base, whether it was the combination of disenfranchised Brooklyn Dodgers and New York Giants fans that came aboard after their respected clubs relocated to the West Coast at the end of the 1950s, or the mix of the various diverse ethnic communities in Queens and beyond the five boroughs in recent years.

The notorious on-field struggles of "Marvelous" Marv Throneberry and the original '62 club under craggy-faced yet twinkle-eyed skipper Casey Stengel instilled Mets partisans with a self-deprecating sense of humor. When

combined with the fans' love of the National League's intellectual style of play, it created a representative New York fan: smart, sarcastic and full of passion.

Although the peaks of the 1969 and 1986 seasons produced two World Series crowns — and two of the most written about teams in Big League annals — Mets fans recount the bitter as often as the sweet, and view suffering through down times as a rite of passage. After all, there's nothing as amazin' as a come-from-behind win.

CITI THAT NEVER SLEEPS

Unlike its oft-maligned, multipurpose predecessor, Shea Stadium, Citi Field is an eye-pleasing park that provides an intimate baseball viewing experience with top-notch amenities at every turn.

Fans emerging from the No. 7 subway train are greeted by the Home Run Apple. A fixture at Shea, it rose after each homer by the Mets but was replaced with a new apple when the team moved next door to Citi Field. To enter the park, most fans will pass through the Jackie Robinson Rotunda, a tribute to the pioneering player who broke the game's color barrier just a few miles away in

PLANES, TRAINS & AUTOMOBILES

This is one city where it's best to buy a Metrocard and leave the rental car behind. Taxis pop up on every street corner, buses are always in service and the subway runs 24 hours a day. The subway is the cheapest, most efficient way to get around the city, with stops convenient to both Citi Field and Yankee Stadium. For those coming from the suburbs, Metro North and the Long Island Railroad also service Yankee Stadium and Citi Field, respectively.

Punctuated by the Empire State building, the Manhattan skyline is one-of-a-kind.

1947. Framed by brick archways and featuring a terrazzo floor, the Rotunda is part of a design that pays tribute to Brooklyn's Ebbets Field. Before heading upstairs to the seats and dining areas, check out the Mets Hall of Fame and Museum, which is located adjacent to the Rotunda and allows fans to catch a glimpse of the club's World Series trophies, Tom Seaver's Cy Young Award and other keepsakes.

Once inside the park, visitors may get so caught up in the diverse food options that they forget they're at a ballgame and not one of Manhattan's finest restaurants. The Taste of New York

food alley features barbecue from Blue Smoke, tacos by the chef at Tabla and burgers, hot dogs, fries and shakes from Shake Shack, all part of a deal with famed restaurateur Danny Meyer.

PROUD IN PINSTRIPES

Depending on one's zip code, there are a lot of differing opinions about Yankees fans. The late comedian Joe E. Lewis famously said, "Rooting for the Yankees is like rooting for U.S. Steel." But dissenting views certainly seem irrelevant when a game begins in the Bronx and the fans in the bleachers begin their traditional "roll call" of the Yankees in the field, which inspires each player to quickly acknowledge the cheer.

Of course, the relievers in the visiting bullpen may not receive as warm a welcome, but there's no doubting the passion of the "bleacher creatures." Among the team's more understated fans are actor Billy Crystal and former New York Mayor Rudy Giuliani, who can be spotted along with any number of visiting celebrities passing through town, including actor Denzel Washington.

Before heading into Yankee Stadium to root for the beloved home team, Bombers fans often can be found congregating at various watering holes

WHAT'S IN A NAME?

When the Metropolitan Baseball Club, Inc. needed a name for its new team, franchise matriarch Joan Payson considered the headlines. After passing on the likes of the Islanders and the Jets (which eventually found their way into the New York sports lexicon anyway, thanks to the NHL and NFL), Payson selected Mets — short for Metropolitans, and at just four letters, a true headline writer's delight.

The team mascot, Mr. Met (left), is beloved by fans. The 1969 Miracle Mets took Game 4 of the World Series, and would go on to win the title as an underdog over Baltimore.

and hole-in-the-wall taverns up and down River Avenue.

THE CATHEDRAL

When the new Yankee Stadium opened in 2009, fans were blown away by how two things so alike could be so different. At field level, the look and feel are the same as the club's old home — but that's about it. Unlike the original Yankee Stadium, built in 1923 and remodeled from 1974–75, the new version features open plazas and concourses, modern technology and high-end restaurants.

Architects recreated the original design's gothic exterior, rebuilt a team museum and expanded Monument Park, which honors Yankee greats. The signature feature is a 31,000-square-foot Great Hall that feels like a baseball version of Grand Central Station.

Old Yankee Stadium was notorious for its lack of dining options. For the new park, the club created its own concession arm: Legends Hospitality.

Restaurants such as Johnny Rockets and Brother Jimmy's BBQ are on site. Full-service dining is also available at Hard Rock Cafe and NYY Steak.

AROUND GOTHAM

Change is a constant in the Big Apple. The city never stops growing, adapting or moving forward. This drive has left little remnant of Hilltop Park or the Polo Grounds in Washington Heights.

Although such landmarks are long gone, one of the few things that hasn't changed is the city's passion for baseball. Until his death in 1995, Mickey Mantle appeared regularly at his namesake restaurant at 42 Central Park South, which is still a popular spot.

Visitors can pay respects to baseball greats about 25 miles north of the city at the Gate of Heaven Cemetery, the final resting place of Babe Ruth and Billy Martin. About a four-hour drive north is the National Baseball Hall of Fame and Museum in Cooperstown.

WHAT'S IN A NAME?

Baseball's winningest franchise, once known as the Baltimore Orioles, moved to New York in 1903 and became the Highlanders, named after its field at Hilltop Park. Newspapers developed the name Yankees from the park's red, white and blue flags, and the name stuck after a move to the Polo Grounds.

Groundskeepers at Yankee Stadium tend to the field (above), and fans walk through the Great Hall in April 2009 — the first month of what would be a championship season.

Closer to the city, the Class-A New York-Penn League features two teams in the five boroughs: the Mets' Brooklyn Cyclones and the Staten Island Yankees.

24/7
New York City earned it's reputation as the "City That Never Sleeps" because

there is so much to do — at any hour. Where to begin? Newcomers often start with the Empire State Building, Statue of Liberty or Rockefeller Center. A boat tour around Manhattan is also a terrific way to get an overview of the city's sights.

Many visitors head downtown to take a picture with the Wall Street bull

statue or to pay tribute at Ground Zero. The Financial District is also the site of the Canyon of Heroes parade route for sports champions and other dignitaries.

Tourists can score tickets for a Broadway musical or TV show taping. One could spend hours just watching the hustle and bustle of Times Square,

shopping or visiting museums. To get away from it all, head to Central Park for a walk or jog. Wherever you go, keep your eyes open. No trip to New York is complete without a celebrity sighting.

There are dozens of neighborhoods and cuisines to explore, including Chinatown and Little Italy. There are film festivals and hundreds of comedy clubs, bars, lounges and music clubs to suit any taste — 24 hours a day.

If baseball doesn't offer enough of a sports fix, there's always an event at Madison Square Garden, the home of the Knicks, Rangers and WNBA Liberty, as well as world-class boxing and concerts.

Fans can visit Times Square (left) and take the 4 train (top) to Yankee Stadium. Citi Field offers terrific food options.

Philadelphia

Philadelphia served as the home of the First Continental Congress in 1774 and the location of the signing of the Declaration of Independence two years later. Yet a less-heralded happening in 1883 may be the bit of local history that currently inspires the most pride around The City of Brotherly Love. That year, in the twilight of the 19th century, the Philadelphia Phillies joined the fledgling National League.

FRONT AND CENTER

From the National League organization's early days at Recreation Park and the Baker Bowl to Shibe Park, the Vet and now Citizens Bank Park, the Philadelphia Phillies are one of the oldest continuous franchises in all of professional sports. Of course, in the early days of the 20th century it was an American League club — the Philadelphia Athletics — that was the top team in town.

At 38 years old, with just three seasons of managerial experience, Connie Mack accepted the job at the helm of the fledgling A's club in 1901, along with a 25 percent ownership stake in the team. Always topped with a straw hat and nattily attired in suit jacket and tie, the gentlemanly Mack would be a fixture in the Athletics' dugout for the next half century.

In 1909, the Athletics began playing at Shibe Park in North Philadelphia, a concrete and steel structure that departed from the wooden ballpark trend of its time. Mack helped design the park, which became known as Connie Mack Stadium in 1953. With a brick and stone facade, it was an architectural masterpiece.

To keep the team financially solvent, Mack traded some of his better players over the years, including Lefty Grove and Jimmie Foxx, which contributed to some of the team's many last-place finishes. In between, however, were stretches of dominance, including three world championships between 1910 and 1913. They also won three straight AL pennants from 1929–31, winning the World Series in 1929 and 1930. The Phillies, meanwhile, played in just one World Series from their inception — which they lost to Boston in 1915 — until 1950 when the upstart "Whiz Kids" captured the NL pennant.

The Athletics moved to Kansas City after the 1954 season, leaving Philadelphia with just the Phillies, who moved into the multipurpose Veterans Stadium along with the NFL's Eagles in 1971. After being swept in the 1950 World Series, the Phillies didn't reach the postseason again until '76. Led by Steve Carlton and Mike Schmidt, the Phillies reached the playoffs six times in eight seasons.

Another playoff drought followed before the club, playing in Citizens Bank Park, began a new era of dominance with the 2008 World Series crown. Thanks to a new generation of stars

including Chase Utley, Ryan Howard and Cole Hamels, the Phillies were able to have a long-awaited victory parade down Broad Street.

BROTHERLY LOVE

Philadelphia fans are notoriously tough. Just ask Santa Claus, who was booed during an Eagles game in 1968. Even Mike Schmidt, perhaps the greatest third baseman ever, caught more than his share of grief from the fans.

Phillies fans have long been partial to unpolished, tough-as-nails players, such as Pete Rose and Larry Bowa. The entire pennant-winning squad of 1993 — which included Lenny Dykstra, John Kruk and Darren Daulton, along with Manager Jim Fregosi — seemed tailor-made for gritty Philly.

Philadelphia's pivotal role in American history is symbolized by Independence Hall (above), the site where the Declaration of Independence and Constitution were created. The Phillie Phanatic (right) is likewise a staple for the city's baseball fans.

The Phillies were perennially one of baseball's best teams from 1976–83, winning the World Series in 1980. But after the Phils lost the Fall Classic in '83, the same year Moses Malone led the NBA's 76ers to an NBA crown, the city's sports teams sunk into a 25-year stretch of mediocrity. The Vet, with its rock-hard AstroTurf and cookie-cutter design, was considered the worst of the multipurpose facilities and only contributed to the hard-knock reputation of Phillies fans.

Still, like fictitious native son Rocky Balboa, Philly faithful reveled in their underdog status, hanging on every word that came from the microphone of Harry Kalas, the team's longtime broadcasting voice.

With the opening of Citizens Bank Park in 2004 and a world title in 2008, the Phillies are no longer underdogs. That hardly makes local fans warm and fuzzy, just a little happier than they were during the leaner years at the Vet.

TAKE IT TO THE BANK
Constructing a Center City ballpark in a neighborhood that is more than 300

PLANES, TRAINS & AUTOMOBILES
The Southeastern Pennsylvania Transit Authority (SEPTA) is an efficient public transportation system, with buses and trains that run throughout the city, including to Citizens Bank Park. Since the stadium has more than 20,000 parking spaces, many fans drive, especially since Philadelphia's base includes supporters from the nearby states of New Jersey and Delaware. Plus, driving in and around Philadelphia isn't nearly as intimidating as in New York, Chicago or Boston. No car? Not to worry. There is mass transit for those coming in from the suburbs.

years old and defined by tiny streets was logistically impossible, so the team found a spot just as suitable — just off the interstate, in the South Philadelphia area that has housed the city's sports teams for years. The former location of home plate at Veterans Stadium is even identified with a granite and bronze marker in the parking lot of Citizens Bank Park.

Opened in 2004, Citizens Bank Park is a hulk of red brick and steel. The giant, neon Liberty Bell behind the center-field wall chimes with every Phillies homer and pays tribute to the famed Liberty Bell that was rung in 1776 to summon citizens to a reading of the Declaration of Independence. Taking a cue from modern ballparks in Denver, Pittsburgh and Atlanta, the Phillies' home stadium features open-air concourses that allow fans a view of the action from anywhere in the park.

Visitors must make sure to see the statues of Phillies greats Robin Roberts, Mike Schmidt and Steve Carlton that are on display outside the stadium.

The Phillies have one of the greatest mascots in sports — the Phanatic — and he appears throughout the stadium on game days. There's the Phanatic Phun Zone for children under 8 located near the first-base gate, as well as a Build-a-Bear Workshop where youngsters can make their own miniature Phanatic.

As far as food goes, Citizens Bank Park has a number of popular eating areas. Ashburn Alley includes Brewerytown, Bull's BBQ and Chickie's and Pete's Crab Fries. Harry the K's Broadcast Bar and Grille, named after the late broadcaster, is located just below the left-field scoreboard. And, as if there was a doubt, Philly cheesesteaks can be had at Campo's and Tony Luke's. McFadden's is also a part of Citizens Bank Park. The restaurant and bar is open during non-game days for fans visiting while the Phils are out of town.

STREETS OF PHILADELPHIA

Few cities offer more to see by foot than Philly does. Take a free "Constitutional Walking Tour" from the Independence Visitor Center through some of the city's most important sites, including

After winning the World Series in 2008, Ryan Howard, Chase Utley (opposite, from left) and the rest of the Phillies made it back to the Fall Classic in 2009. Shibe Park was home to the Philadelphia A's (top). Geno's serves up a must-have cheesesteak in Philly.

Independence Hall, the Liberty Bell Center, City Tavern, Elfreth's Alley and the Betsy Ross House. Visitors can see where founding fathers John Adams, Benjamin Franklin, Thomas Jefferson and George Washington laid out the blueprints of the new republic. The route includes more than 30 historic sites and passes by numerous shops and restaurants should you get the urge for some modern trappings.

Franklin Square is one of the five public squares that William Penn laid out in his original plan for the city, and it boasts several new, family-friendly attractions including a miniature golf course, a classic carousel, storytelling benches and a picnic area.

Along the banks of the Schuylkill River you'll find scenic paths to walk, bike or blade while watching the rowing of a variety of local crew teams. Penn's Landing, on the nearby Delaware River, hosts many festivals and concerts as well as a dock of tall ships and the Independence Seaport Museum. In the summer, Phlash, a purple trolley, brings visitors to 20 key destinations across the city.

No trip to the City of Brotherly Love would be complete without a visit to the Philadelphia Art Museum. Cue the "Rocky" theme on your iPod and make the cinematic dash up the steps — shadowboxing optional. For another cliche, but must-have Philly experience, head over to rivals Pat's or Geno's to try two of the most famous cheesesteaks in the world.

Citizens Bank Park is a must see.

Baltimore

Situated along the Patapsco River, which flows into the Chesapeake Bay, Baltimore's appearance, cuisine and culture has been affected a great deal by its role as a major U.S. seaport. Featuring now-rejuvenated industrial warehouses and a plethora of distinct neighborhoods, Baltimore is a swinging door between the South and Northeast, with plenty of stories to tell — especially on the diamond.

CHARM CITY

All eyes were on Camden Yards on Sept. 6, 1995, as a record long thought to be unbreakable was about to be shattered by Cal Ripken Jr. When that game between the Orioles and Angels became official after the top half of the fifth, it put Ripken's consecutive-games-played streak at 2,131. One of the most joyous moments in Big League annals took place as Ripken celebrated breaking Lou Gehrig's iron-man mark.

"It was an out-of-body experience," Ripken recalled. "It's like when your wife is having a baby. You're thinking, 'This can't be me. This can't be my wife. This can't be my child.' I kept thinking, 'This can't be happening to me. This has to be someone else.'"

From Ripken's record-breaking streak all the way back to 1882 when the Orioles became a charter member of the American Association, few communities have as long and storied a history with baseball as Charm City. After the upstart AA folded in 1891, the Orioles joined the National League. Future Hall of Famers Wee Willie Keeler, John McGraw, Wilbert Robinson and Hughie Jennings wreaked havoc under Manager Ned Hanlon and three consecutive pennants flew over Baltimore from 1894–96.

Although the NL eliminated the Orioles and three other teams following the 1899 campaign, McGraw, a second-year player-manager, formed a new Orioles team in the fledgling American League beginning in 1901. After just two seasons in Baltimore, that club moved to New York, becoming the Highlanders and later the Yankees. From 1903–53, another incarnation of local Orioles competed in what is now the Triple-A level, giving a start to Baltimore native George Herman Ruth, who pitched for the Orioles before being sold to the Red Sox in 1914.

The St. Louis Browns moved to Baltimore for the 1954 season and, unlike most relocated teams of the time, settled on a familiar name. These Orioles emerged as a pennant contender in the mid-1960s thanks to one of the game's most fearsome pitching staffs — featuring aces Jim Palmer, Dave McNally and Mike Cuellar — and the superb play of Brooks and Frank Robinson (no relation). The Orioles won the 1966 World Series and played in the postseason six times in the next decade. The club also won the World Series in 1983, Ripken's second season, and later enjoyed a renaissance along with the city's Inner Harbor, thanks in part to Camden Yards in the 1990s.

TAKING FLIGHT

Shortly after arriving from St. Louis in 1954, the Orioles were embraced by baseball fans that hadn't had a Major League team since 1915. The team's rise and subsequent AL dominance during the glory years of the 1960s cemented its local status, and a number of off-the-field factors ensured that the regional fan base only grew.

When the Washington Senators left the nation's capital after 1971, the Orioles expanded their reach south. And when the NFL's Baltimore Colts departed for Indianapolis after the 1983 season, the Orioles became the Chesapeake region's only major sports franchise until Art Modell moved his Cleveland Browns to town to become the Ravens in 1996. In the interim, the team opened Oriole Park at Camden Yards, inspiring a spate of back-to-the-future baseball stadiums around the country that combine classic architecture with modern amenities.

Taking their cue from the likes of savvy star skippers Earl Weaver and Davey Johnson and intellectual players such as Eddie Murray, Jim Palmer and Cal Ripken Jr., Baltimore fans tend to be a cerebral bunch. Although the Orioles don't have the national following of their AL East competitors in New York or Boston, they held their own on the field and financially with the Yankees and Red Sox for much of the 1990s, reaching the ALCS in 1997.

GOING YARDS

Since Oriole Park at Camden Yards opened in 1992, 18 Major League ballparks have been built, many aiming to replicate its cozy, retro feel.

Eutaw Street (opposite) is a bustling scene on game days. A seaport, Baltimore boasts famous crab (top) and one of the largest aquariums in the country.

PLANES, TRAINS & AUTOMOBILES

Camden Station, adjacent to Camden Yards, connects the baseball stadium to the Baltimore-Washington International Airport and Washington D.C. via MARC commuter rail service and local light rail trains. Given the location of BWI halfway between Baltimore and D.C., rental cars are a must for visitors looking to explore Baltimore beyond the Inner Harbor.

Many have mimicked the brick aesthetic of Camden Yards, but it's impossible to duplicate the 1,116-foot-long B&O Warehouse beyond the right-field wall — the longest building on the East Coast. Eutaw Street, the pedestrian walkway between the warehouse and outfield, gives the ballpark a neighborhood feel.

Built on an old railroad center just two blocks from the birthplace of Babe Ruth, Camden Yards oozes charm and history. The Babe's father operated Ruth's Cafe on the ground floor of the family residence located at Conway Street and Little Paca, now center field at Oriole Park.

During many Orioles home games, Boog Powell, the former All-Star first baseman for the O's, can usually be found signing autographs and serving up tasty dishes at Boog's BBQ, which is located beneath a green tent behind the center-field bleachers on Eutaw Street. If BBQ isn't on your menu, then don't forget that Maryland is also famous for its crab cakes.

THE HOUSE WHERE RUTH WAS BORN

The Babe Ruth Birthplace and Museum, just minutes from Camden Yards, chronicles the Bambino's life and even includes the room in which he was born. Another nearby place to take in some of Maryland's sports lore is the Sports Legends Museum at Camden Yards. Owned and operated by the Babe Ruth Birthplace and Museum, it occupies the basement and first floor of Camden Station, adjacent to the park.

If Ruth is Baltimore's most famous native son, then Cal Ripken Jr. may be its most beloved adopted one. Ripken built a 110-acre baseball complex 45 minutes west of the city in Aberdeen that includes Ripken Stadium, home to the Class-A Aberdeen Ironbirds, and many youth baseball and softball fields. The Cal Ripken World Series is played on youth fields modeled after Camden Yards, Baltimore's Memorial Stadium, Fenway Park and Wrigley Field.

SAFE HARBOR

Oriole Park at Camden Yards helped revitalize Baltimore's Inner Harbor, which as recently as 20 years ago consisted mostly of run-down warehouses. Now, it's a must-see spot and includes the National Aquarium, Maryland Science Center, and many restaurants and shops. Also worth visiting is Fort McHenry, where Francis Scott Key penned "The Star-Spangled Banner" as U.S. troops defended the harbor during the War of 1812. The Harbor is still a working port and it's possible to see the area via sailboat tours, water taxis and boat rentals.

Geppi's Entertainment Museum, created by Orioles part-owner Steve Geppi, contains thousands of comic books, films and exhibits. It's located on the second floor of Camden Station.

At Port Discovery — Baltimore's children's museum — kids and adults can explore the three-story KidWorks, a space-age jungle gym featuring slides, ropes, stairs, zip-lines and tunnels.

Nearby Fells Point is popular for bars and nightclubs. Federal Hill is home to dozens of restaurants, bars and boutiques. It's one of the oldest areas of town and was popular back in the days of the master of the "macabre," Edgar Allan Poe. Once a hot spot of the city's maritime trade industry, Federal Hill is now an up-and-coming residential and entertainment district catering to a young professional crowd.

WHAT'S IN A NAME?

In 1901, the franchise was founded as the Milwaukee Brewers, but moved to St. Louis and became the Browns the next year. After a dismal 1953 season, the team left Missouri. Arriving in Baltimore, the club dubbed itself the Orioles after Maryland's state bird.

Brooks Robinson (above) offered his fielding prowess to the Orioles for 23 seasons, a long and beloved career similar to that of Cal Ripken Jr. (right), who played 21 years in Baltimore, and set baseball's consecutive games played mark with the team in 1995.

Washington, D.C.

The nation's capital crackles with energy and sometimes controversy, its population expanding by more than 1 million during the work week. It's impossible to ignore the influence of politics on every aspect of life in Washington D.C., including baseball. When U.S. President William Howard Taft threw out the first pitch on Opening Day 1910, he started a tradition that has linked the White House and the Majors for a century.

THE DISTRICT

"First in war, first in peace, last in the American League." So went the line about Washington during the 1950s and '60s. The Senators' run of futility in their final years in Washington, D.C., obscured the fact they were actually one of the most successful franchises from 1912–33. The team's roster included future Hall of Famers Goose Goslin, Joe Cronin, Heinie Manush, Sam Rice and Walter "The Big Train" Johnson. The club won the Fall Classic in 1924, and appeared in the Series in 1925 and '33.

Calvin Griffith moved the Senators to Minnesota after 1960, but an expansion team arrived the next year, playing one season at Griffith Stadium before moving to what would later be named Robert F. Kennedy Memorial Stadium.

The 1960s Senators, headlined by slugger Frank Howard and skippers Gil Hodges and Ted Williams, posted just one winning season (1969, under Williams) before Owner Bob Short moved the team to Texas in 1972, where it became the Rangers. Major League action didn't return until 2005, when the MLB-owned Montreal Expos were relocated to the country's capital and rebranded as the Nationals.

Big League play returned to RFK Stadium for three seasons while a new ballpark was built along the Anacostia River. President George W. Bush threw out the first pitch to open Nationals Park in 2008. Such ceremonial tosses unite all eras of Washington baseball. It's those early, dominant years of Beltway baseball, though, with which today's Nationals are hoping to reconnect. With sluggers like Adam Dunn joining forces with homegrown talent like Ryan Zimmerman and Stephen Strasburg, it looks as if the District can hope for a team to match the town's national authority.

THE NATIONALS PASTIME

D.C. officials hope Nationals Park will be the impetus for economic development in the historic Anacostia area in Southeast Washington, much like Coors Field revitalized Denver's "LoDo" district and Camden Yards jump-started a renaissance for Baltimore's Inner Harbor.

Nationals Park lacks views of all of the city's landmarks, but makes up for it by providing fans with ideal sightlines and plenty of vantage points to view the game while inside the park.

The Nationals cater to families, and not just with affordable seating. The

PLANES, TRAINS & AUTOMOBILES

With almost 90 stations in the city and surrounding suburbs, Washington's Metro rail system provides easy-to-navigate transportation. It goes to Reagan International Airport and offers an easy alternative to driving through the city's congested streets. The Navy Yard stop on the Green Line is less than a block from Nationals Park.

If you are traveling by car, you may find yourself on the "Beltway," a stretch of I-495 that circles the capital and its inner suburbs in Maryland and Virginia. Notorious for traffic, the Beltway also gives the insular political city its nickname.

The U.S. Capitol building, Washington Monument, Lincoln Memorial and National Mall (left) are a historical juxtaposition to young Nats like Ryan Zimmerman (above, center).

"Rushmore" mascots — George Washington, Thomas Jefferson, Abraham Lincoln and Theodore Roosevelt — mingle with fans during games. Their images are everywhere and they engage in a race between innings, just like the popular sausages in Milwaukee.

WASHINGTON'S MONUMENTS

Washington is rich in attractions and sights. The National Mall is a hub, with memorials to Abraham Lincoln, Thomas Jefferson and Franklin Delano Roosevelt, along with those who were lost in World War II, Korea and Vietnam. There's the U.S. Capitol building, the Washington Monument and the Smithsonian National Air & Space Museum, National Gallery of Art and U.S. Holocaust Memorial Museum. Tours of the White House are available, but requests must be submitted up to six months in advance.

Symbolically linking the north and the south of the city is the Memorial Bridge. It's aligned between the Lincoln Memorial and Arlington House, which is the Robert E. Lee Memorial and gateway to Arlington National Cemetery.

Another must-see is Georgetown. During the day, it's a historic district and home to its namesake university, but at night, it's a social hub, where the ambitious and powerful go to be seen.

Take the kids to the National Zoo that borders Rock Creek Park in the upper northwest portion of the city. It offers free admission, and also has a convenient Metro stop (Woodley Park/Zoo).

George Washington's Mount Vernon plantation in Alexandria, Va., is more than worth the 30-minute drive. It's a pleasant trip along the scenic George Washington Parkway south of Reagan International and Old Town Alexandria.

WHAT'S IN A NAME?

Three of the baseball teams previously based in our nation's capital had named themselves, patriotically, the Nationals. After a 36-year stint as the Montreal Expos, the latest Major League team to settle in Washington selected this familiar moniker as well. However, they went about the selection in a modern way, choosing based on data from focus groups.

Visitors should definitely make plans to visit the White House while in D.C. Pitching prodigy Stephen Strasburg (right) drew a world of attention when he debuted in 2010.

chapter 6

the heartland

PITTSBURGH

CLEVELAND

CINCINNATI

ST. LOUIS

KANSAS CITY

Pittsburgh

Founded at the confluence of the Allegheny, Monongahela and Ohio rivers, Pittsburgh is a quintessential boomtown, and hardworking folks in the "Steel City" join together when it comes to their sports teams. It's a one-team-per-sport town and the Pirates, Steelers and Penguins each don black and gold. The harsh winters, blue-collar backgrounds and like-minded rooting interests all make this a tight-knit community.

THE CITY OF CHAMPIONS

Pittsburgh didn't just send its hometown team to the inaugural World Series in 1903; in many baseball circles the "Steel City" is considered to have invented the Fall Classic. In 1903, Pirates Owner Barney Dreyfuss wrote a letter to the owner of the American League's Boston Americans suggesting that his NL pennant–winning club take on the top AL team in a "World's Series." Although Boston edged Pittsburg (which was spelled without the 'h' back then) in eight games, it was just a few years before the Pirates were back competing for the title.

The Pittsburg Alleghenies had joined the American Association in 1882, and built Exposition Park where the Allegheny, Monongahela and Ohio rivers converge. This site would later become home to Three Rivers Stadium and PNC Park. After being renamed the Pirates in 1891, repeated flooding forced the club to move to Forbes Field, a new steel and concrete facility. Forbes Field hosted the inaugural Fall Classic as well as the 1909 Series, in which the Pirates, led by shortstop Honus Wagner, beat Ty Cobb's Detroit Tigers in seven games.

Max Carey and Pie Traynor led the Bucs to the World Series in 1925, where they took the crown, and again in 1927, where they lost to the Ruth-Gehrig Yankees. Pittsburgh would not return to the Series again until 1960, when light-hitting, defensive whiz Bill Mazeroski smacked a ball over the ivy-covered left-field wall of Forbes Field against the New York Yankees in Game 7, becoming the first player to hit a World Series–ending home run.

The 1970s included the saddest of the city's sports moments: On Dec. 31, 1972, Hall of Fame Pirates outfielder Roberto Clemente died in a plane crash while attempting to deliver relief supplies to earthquake victims in Nicaragua. Despite that tragic loss, the Bucs were among the most successful teams of the 1970s, winning six NL East titles and World Series championships in 1971 and '79.

Between the Pirates and Steelers, Three Rivers Stadium was the meeting place for "The City of Champions" in the '70s with the "We Are Family" Pirates of Willie Stargell, Bill Madlock and Dave Parker finishing the decade wearing the World Series crown. A decade later, Jim Leyland and Barry Bonds led the Pirates to three straight NL East titles (1990–92). In 2001, Pittsburgh opened PNC Park. Modeled after Forbes Field, the ballpark became an instant classic, a perfect tribute to the city's rich baseball history.

A PIRATE LIFE

There might not be a more closely bound group of fans anywhere than Pittsburgh. This holds true even though the Pirates have struggled since the breakup of teams led by Barry Bonds, Bobby Bonilla and Andy Van Slyke during the late 1980s and early 1990s. Older Bucs fans still reminisce about Forbes Field, and can tell you where they were when Bill Mazeroski hit his World Series walk-off shot in 1960. Middle-aged fans remember singing along to Sister Sledge in 1979 and being part of Willie "Pops" Stargell's "family." Younger fans remember the heartbreak of the seven-game loss to the Braves and Francisco Cabrera in the 1992 NLCS, and fans of all ages still look to Roberto Clemente as a symbol of hope even years after his untimely passing.

Bucs fans have embraced quirky pitchers such as Jim Rooker, Bert Blyleven, John Candelaria, Bob Walk and Denny Neagle, while showing little patience for players who don't hustle. The front office has gone after gritty men like Danny Murtaugh, Phil "Scrap Iron" Garner, Jim Leyland and Doug Drabek, who fit perfectly with the city and team.

Inspired by a great history and one of the game's best ballparks, the Pittsburgh fanbase remains unfailingly loyal to its city and team.

RIVERS-FRONT VIEW

Pirates fans take great pride in having such a picturesque home field. Built along the Allegheny River on the site of the team's first home, Exposition Park, PNC Park is

PLANES, TRAINS & AUTOMOBILES

It's possible to drive or take a boat to PNC Park, although many walk across the scenic Roberto Clemente Bridge that spans the Allegheny River. Pittsburgh is a great pedestrian town with many attractions packed together. But for a bigger city, it's not hard to navigate or find parking.

PNC Park (left) in Pittsburgh (top) is one of baseball's most scenic spots. It was built to honor Forbes Field, site of Bill Mazeroski's (above) 1960 homer.

cozy (38,496 fans) and honors Forbes Field with its brick exterior and masonry arches.

The park provides fans with a breathtaking view of the downtown Pittsburgh skyline, and a relaxed setting that can feel as cozy as Spring Training or a Minor League park. Many fans walk to the stadium by way of the Roberto Clemente Bridge. Once across, visitors are just steps from a Clemente statue, which depicts the great right fielder in the follow-through of his swing. Similarly, Hall of Famers Willie Stargell and Honus Wagner are immortalized with statues at other entrances to the park.

Gastronomically speaking, the food offerings at PNC are limitless. Pops' Plaza, named for Willie Stargell, is located on the third-base side of the main concourse and serves gyros, "Pops' Potato Patch" (fresh cut French Fries with a variety of toppings) and Pub 475, which pours local brews.

Primanti Brothers offers the famous Primanti sandwich — grilled meat, cheese, tomatoes, cole slaw and French fries on Italian bread. The sandwich dates back to the Great Depression, when Joe Primanti and his nephew, John, first served sandwiches from a wooden lunch stand in Pittsburgh's famed Strip District.

Manny's Bar-B-Q, located on the Riverwalk behind center field, features barbecue specials from former Bucs catcher Manny Sanguillen, who, like Boog Powell in Baltimore, is usually on hand signing autographs.

FALLEN BUT NOT FORGOTTEN
The Roberto Clemente Museum features thousands of Clemente items, along with original seats from Forbes Field, remnants of which still stand in and around the University of

Pittsburgh's Posvar Hall, just off Forbes Avenue. The portion of the left-field wall of Forbes, over which Bill Mazeroski hit his famous home run, is outlined in brick in the pavement. Fans gather on Oct. 13 each year at the site to commemorate the dramatic end to the 1960 World Series. For more Bucs history, the Senator John Heinz Regional History Center dedicates two floors to the Pirates as well as the rest of Pittsburgh's sports teams.

THE CITY OF BRIDGES
Point State Park is in the heart of the city where the three rivers join. For a bird's eye view of the city and the confluence, take the Monongahela or Duquesne trams up Mount Washington.

To fit in some family fun, Pittsburgh features one of the few combination zoo and aquariums in America. The 77-acre facility features thousands of animals and sea critters. There's also the

National Aviary, home to more than 600 exotic birds from all seven continents.

Museum lovers can choose from the Children's Museum, Carnegie Museum of Art or Fort Pitt Museum, which chronicles the city's history. The Andy Warhol Museum is dedicated to the late pop art icon and Pittsburgh native.

Pittsburgh is a great city for walking, as it has several distinct neighborhoods to explore. The Strip District is a mile-long stretch that offers markets and antique shops by day and a pulsing nightlife after dark. Just beyond the banks of the Monongahela River is the South Side, an area known for its diverse population and recent boom in dining and shopping that brings together a variety of eras and personalities. The Oakland neighborhood is the favorite of the local college crowd, while the Cultural District is home to live music venues, including the famous Heinz Hall Theater.

WHAT'S IN A NAME?
The Pirates' moniker is more an accusation than a tribute. When the weak Players' League folded after the 1890 season, Pittsburgh's Innocents were thrilled that Louis Bierbauer signed with them instead of returning to his Philadelphia Athletics. The A's were furious, accusing Pittsburgh of "pirating" Bierbauer. The not-so-Innocents held onto him — and the new nickname.

Primanti Brothers employees at PNC Park (top) make Pittsburgh's trademark Primanti sandwiches, which date back to the Great Depression. Fans and locals walk across the Roberto Clemente Bridge (right), which spans the Allegheny River in downtown Pittsburgh.

NEXT HOME GAME
OCT. 24TH
WE BELIEVE

Cleveland

At the crossroads of where the East Coast meets the Midwest, Cleveland's cultural diversity and attractions, paired with its location on the southern shore of Lake Erie, make it a scenic, urban and recreational destination. Considering its size, there are few cities that can rival Cleveland for finding a good time. When it comes to sports, the Ohio city's faithful fans are truly on the same team regardless of results.

ALONG THE SHORES OF THE CUYAHOGA

One of the eight charter members of the American League in 1901, Cleveland's Major League club had played under a variety of monikers — Blues, Bronchos and Naps — before ownership decided on Indians after the 1914 season, perhaps hoping to replicate the popularity of the Boston Braves.

But it wasn't until 1920 that the Tribe won its first world championship under player-manager Tris Speaker. The title, though, was tinged with sadness. On Aug. 16 of that year, Yankees pitcher Carl Mays hit Indians shortstop Ray Chapman in the head with a pitch, fracturing his skull. Chapman died the next day, becoming the only Major League player to sustain a fatal injury from a pitched ball.

The Indians did not win another World Series until 1948. That season, Owner Bill Veeck unleashed quite a few outlandish promotional stunts, delighting fans and infuriating league officials. Not surprisingly, the Tribe drew huge crowds to Cleveland's massive Municipal Stadium.

A key member of the 1948 squad was Larry Doby, who had broken the AL color barrier in 1947 and hit at a .301 clip in '48, his first full season in the Majors. Late in the year, Veeck signed another Negro Leagues star, legendary pitcher Satchel Paige, and the Tribe won the Fall Classic in six games over the Boston Braves.

Cleveland returned to the World Series in 1954 after winning a franchise-record 111 games. The '54 club, helmed by Manager Al Lopez, fielded one of the best starting rotations ever: Bob Lemon, Bob Feller, Early Wynn, Mike Garcia and Art Houtteman. The quintet combined for a 2.91 ERA, racking up 93 wins during the regular season. The favored Indians, though, could not overcome the Giants, who won the title in a four-game sweep highlighted by Willie Mays' over-the-shoulder

catch off the bat of Vic Wertz in Game 1 at the Polo Grounds.

After decades of struggles, Owner Richard Jacobs and General Manager John Hart assembled a talented young team just in time for the opening of Jacobs Field (now Progressive Field) in 1994. Thanks to sluggers Jim Thome, Manny Ramirez and David Justice, the slick-fielding Omar Vizquel and speedy Kenny Lofton, the Tribe brought home the AL pennant in 1995 and '97, but fell short of the world title both times.

MEMBERS OF THE TRIBE

After being one of the most dominant teams in the American League in the 1940s and '50s, the Indians fell on hard times — for the next four decades. In some places, such a stretch would

Cleveland faithful cheer during the 1995 World Series (left). Arguably the Tribe's biggest fan, John Adams (above) is known for his drum-pounding.

have forced a team to pick up and relocate, but in Cleveland it became a common bond among fans, even inspiring the 1989 hit baseball comedy *Major League* starring Charlie Sheen.

It was never as lonely in the stands at old Municipal Stadium as portrayed in the movie *Major League* — which was actually filmed at Milwaukee's smaller County Stadium — but there was no mistaking the sea change by Lake Erie when the club opened its new park — then known as Jacobs Field — in 1994.

When 41,485 Indians fans packed "the Jake" on June 12, 1995, the city and the team embarked on a six-year sellout streak that would last more than 450 games. Fans seem to appreciate the Tribe's success more after so many years of struggle. Nobody is a bigger fan than John Adams, who has sat in

the bleachers pounding a large bass drum since 1973. Adams' drum reverberates through the ballpark, inciting a chorus of rhythmic clapping.

Although Adams may be a one-man band at Progressive Field, "Grady's Ladies" buy tickets en masse. A group of local women dedicated to Indians centerfielder Grady Sizemore, the clan has grown from just five ladies to more than 300. Members can often be found rooting on the home team and the hunky slugger from Progressive Field's bleachers.

MAKING PROGRESS

"The Jake," known today as Progressive Field, was part of the first wave of retro ballparks constructed around the Majors following the opening of Camden Yards in Baltimore. At Progressive, there are numerous nooks and crannies that

encourage fans to stand together and watch the game when not in their seats.

There's a lifelike statue of Hall of Famer Bob Feller, an eight-time All-Star and perennial Cleveland icon, beyond center field. The Indians' ballpark is part of the downtown Gateway Complex, which also includes Quicken Loans Arena (formerly Gund Arena), home to the NBA's Cleveland Cavaliers.

Visitors stumbling upon Progressive Field by accident can catch a glimpse of the game for free from a plaza beyond left field. Once inside, Progressive Field offers a vast array of cuisine, including sushi, Cuban sandwiches, Mexican fare and traditional ballpark favorites. Some prefer to dine in a glass-enclosed restaurant, others from the highest bleacher seat. Whether watching the game or the skyline, the views are always outstanding.

CARD SHARPS

Sports fans descend on Cleveland when the National Sports Collectors Convention comes to town. It's the largest memorabilia show anywhere.

Any fans wishing to visit Cleveland Municipal Stadium must settle for a football game at Cleveland Browns Stadium, which sits on the site of the Tribe's old home. Pieces of the demolished facility serve as an artificial reef in Lake Erie.

The Indians' Double-A club, the Akron Aeros of the Eastern League, play just 40 miles from the Indians' home, in Canal Park in Akron, Ohio, which was built by the same architectural firm that designed Progressive Field.

ROCK ON

Every Friday night, just around quitting time, Cleveland radio station WMMS used to play Ian Hunter's "Cleveland Rocks." The high-octane rock-and-roll song became a de facto anthem for the town, gracing the opening credits of local comedian Drew Carey's sitcom and blaring over the public address system after countless sporting victories along the Cuyahoga. Fittingly, the Rock and Roll Hall of Fame and Museum is located in downtown Cleveland. Give yourself plenty of time to take in the museum's many exhibit halls and films.

Just four miles east of the downtown area, University Circle is home to many of the city's top attractions, including the Cleveland Botanical Garden and the Cleveland Museum of Art. The latter features 40,000 pieces in its collection, including masterpieces by Monet, Picasso and Van Gogh.

Head to the shores of Lake Erie to visit the *USS Cod* submarine, which took out a convoy of Japanese vessels in World War II. Unlike other restored subs

that have added stairways and doors to the pressure hull for public access, visitors use the same vertical ladders and hatches once used by the crew.

Cleveland has its own niche neighborhoods, too. Little Italy is a great place for pizza, pasta or artwork. Coventry Village provides a taste of 1960s style counterculture, while the Tremont area offers some of the best restaurants and pubs in town.

One of Cleveland's top draws is the Rock and Roll Hall of Fame and Museum (left), located in the city's downtown area. Indians stars have included Satchel Paige and Larry Doby (top, from left) in the late 1940s, and more recently, Grady Sizemore.

Cincinnati

Located on the cusp of the Midwestern and the Southern states, the Queen City was the first major inland metropolis in the country, and is the product of varied cultural and geographical influences. As a result, Cincinnati can claim a pivotal role in numerous historic events and movements in the United States — from the Civil War and the Civil Rights Movement to the beginnings of our national pastime.

GREAT AMERICAN TALE

The Cincinnati Red Stockings were the first all-professional baseball team in 1869. Soon, other amateur baseball outfits were turning pro in hopes of keeping up with the juggernaut. Already with a proud baseball history, Cincinnati became home to the Reds, a charter member of the National League, in 1876.

Not surprisingly, the first-ever Opening Day festivities were held in Cincinnati in 1889, a tradition that continued deep into the 20th century with Cincinnati staging the first pitch of each baseball season. The list of baseball firsts and one-of-a-kind occurrences extends on the field as well, with the city being the site of the first night game in Major League history, played under the lights of Crosley Field in 1935. In 1938, left-hander Johnny Vander Meer became the only pitcher in baseball history to toss back-to-back no-hitters. The Reds were swept by the Yankees in the 1939 World Series, but returned in 1940 and defeated the Detroit Tigers in seven games.

While baseball initially thrived in the city thanks to players like Harry and George Wright, Edd Roush and Heinie Groh, the '70s would be the defining decade for the Reds. Led by Manager Sparky Anderson and a lineup featuring Pete Rose, Johnny Bench, Joe Morgan, Tony Perez and George Foster, the team was dubbed the "Big Red Machine" and reached the World Series four times that decade, winning twice.

A 14-year title drought would be quenched in 1990 when Manager Lou Piniella led the club to a four-game World Series sweep of the heavily-favored Oakland A's. The Reds reached the postseason again in 1995 behind shortstop and National League MVP Barry Larkin, a Queen City native who graduated from Cincinnati's Moeller High.

After 32 seasons in multipurpose Riverfront Stadium, the Reds moved to Great American Ball Park, which pays tribute to the city's baseball tradition.

RED HOT START

Opening Day is an unofficial civic holiday in Cincinnati, with a parade and with many fans taking the day off from work or school to cheer on the Reds. Even if a game broadcast nationally on Sunday night on ESPN now technically serves as the start of the Major League season, the first pitch of the Reds' opener is still considered the beginning by traditionalists. In fact, the Reds are the only team scheduled to start the year at home every season.

PLANES, TRAINS & AUTOMOBILES

Despite it being a large metropolitan area that sprawls along the north shore of the Ohio River, Cincinnati still has the feel of a small town with Vine Street running north from the Ohio River and bisecting the remaining portion of the city. Even though there is no light rail or subway system in Cincinnati, it's usually possible to get to anywhere in the city within 20 minutes by car. Those behind the wheel will be pleased to know that there is plenty of convenient parking at Great American Ball Park, as well as in the surrounding area along the Ohio River.

Crowds of red are the norm at Great American Ball Park (left). Reds fans flood the streets during the annual Opening Day Parade (above) in downtown Cincinnati.

With such a rich history, Cincinnati fans can be forgiven for coming across as if they invented the game. After all, no city has a longer Major League history. Part of the reason that local fans cherish their Reds is that the city has no NBA or NHL club, and the NFL's Bengals have yet to win a Super Bowl. Cincinnati, like St. Louis and Boston, is first and foremost a baseball town.

Cincinnati is also a close-knit community with a small-town feel. It's why the team has been such a perfect match for native sons Barry Larkin and Ken Griffey Jr., along with upbeat additions like Sean Casey, nicknamed "The Mayor" during his time with the Reds.

The franchise might be best known for the Big Red Machine era, rolling on AstroTurf in Riverfront Stadium wearing pullover jerseys. But the city of Cincinnati has just as often been associated with gray flannel uniforms and classic, old-time baseball.

GREAT AMERICAN PASTIME
Great American Ball Park is named for club sponsor Great American Insurance Group, but the name fits a retro-modern ballpark that honors the club's former home at Crosley Field and Cincinnati's role in America's game.

Crosley Terrace serves as a monument to Crosley Field, with bronze statues of Reds greats Frank Robinson, Ted Kluszewski, Joe Nuxhall and Ernie Lombardi. The grass area of the terrace has the same slope as Crosley Field's outfield terrace.

The "power stacks," located in right-center field, resemble the smokestacks of steamboats that were commonly seen along the Ohio River in the early 20th century. Fireworks are launched from the stacks after every Reds home run and victory.

Like many new stadiums, Great American Ball Park features open concourses and walkways that allow fans to wander throughout the stadium without missing a pitch. And with so much to see, it can be hard for visitors to stay in their seats. Be sure to check out the Reds Hall of Fame and Museum, the Reds Fan Zone and the "4,192" mural on the back of the left-field scoreboard depicting the bat that Pete Rose used to collect his record-setting hit.

For panoramic views of the ballpark and the Ohio River, head up to the Cincinnati Bell Riverboat Deck, located on top of the batter's eye structure on the center-field suite level concourse. After inspecting the park, stop by top food attractions — barbecue from the Montgomery Inn or Skyline Chili.

PAST MEETS FUTURE

Although Great American Ball Park is the home of today's Reds, for nearly a century the franchise played at Crosley Field. The Blue Ash Sports Center, 10 miles northeast of Cincinnati, includes a replica of Crosley Field built from its original blueprints. The field, used by local youth teams, includes the distinctive outfield terrace, same outfield dimensions and 400 original seats.

Some of the kids playing on that field may one day play for Archbishop Moeller High School, the alma mater of Big Leaguers Ken Griffey Jr., Barry Larkin, and Buddy, Mike and David Bell.

Two Hall of Famers have their final resting places in greater Cincinnati. Former Yankees Manager Miller Huggins is buried at the Spring Grove Cemetery and Arboretum, while 19th century Negro Leagues star Buck Ewing rests at Mount Washington Cemetery.

ROAD TO FREEDOM

Next to the Reds' ballpark is the National Underground Railroad Freedom Center. The educational center and museum honors slaves who crossed the Ohio River during the 19th century and abolitionists who helped them.

Cincinnati is also home to the William Howard Taft House, where the 27th President of the United States was born. Aside from its historical sites, Cincinnati is a great place for families and kids. The Kings Island theme park, just 20 minutes north, is known for its daring roller coasters, as well as loads of water rides. The nearby Beach Waterpark is 35 acres of aquatic fun.

The Cincinnati Museum Center at Union Terminal is a four-in-one educational experience housed in a restored Art Deco train station. Visitors can see the Omnimax Theater, along with three museums: the Children's, the Natural

History and Science and the city's History Museum. The Cincinnati Zoo and Botanical, which opened in 1872, is the second-oldest in the U.S., and is home to more than 500 animal species and more than 3,000 plant varieties.

Fountain Square is home to the Tyler Davidson Fountain, one of the city's most recognizable landmarks, and is the symbolic center of the city. With many restaurants and seating areas, it's a popular place for concerts and people watching.

WHAT'S IN A NAME?

Cincinnati's Base Ball Club was first called the Resolutes. When New York cricket player Harry Wright arrived, he was among the first to outfit his players in knicker-style trousers. The short pants exposed red socks, leaving the team colored as the Reds.

The "Big Red Machine" (opposite, from left) boasted Pete Rose, Joe Morgan and Johnny Bench in the lineup. The well-visited Tyler Davidson Fountain is the symbol of the city.

St. Louis

St. Louis is classic Midwest, with friendly faces and sticky summers. But above all, "The Gateway City" is a baseball town. Although the NFL's Rams and the NHL's Blues have had their share of moments in the sun, it's the Cardinals who arouse the passion of St. Louis residents. Others may be louder or more aggressive, but no fanbase in the Major Leagues is more famously loyal to its hometown ballplayers.

GATEWAY TO THE WEST

Stan Musial made his Big League debut with the Cardinals in September 1941, during the end of a heated pennant race with the Brooklyn Dodgers. Although the Redbirds finished second in the NL that year, Musial hit .426 in the final 12 contests. The rest, they say, is history. Musial, dubbed "The Man" for his success at the plate, spent 22 seasons in the Majors, earning three NL MVP Awards, three championships and a mind-blowing 24 selections to the All-Star Game. Known for his humility and unique batting stance, Musial set the tone for the St. Louis Cardinals to be a continual powerhouse.

But long before Musial — and more recently Albert Pujols — St. Louis had a reputation for showmanship befitting its status as the game's Western's frontier. Chris Von

der Ahe, who owned the St. Louis Browns from 1882–98, surrounded Sportsman's Park with an amusement park and ran a beer garden and a horse track on the field of play.

Rebuilt after a series of fires, Sportsman's Park opened as home to the AL's Browns in 1909, and welcomed the NL's Cardinals in 1920. The Cardinals were one of the most successful teams of the era, playing in the World Series nine times between 1926–46, winning six titles.

The St. Louis Browns, however, were not so successful. Flamboyant promoter Bill Veeck, who purchased the team in 1951, tried to compensate for poor play with zany promotions, including sending 3-foot-7 Eddie Gaedel to the plate in August that year. After the 1953 season, Veeck sold the team and it was moved to Baltimore, becoming the Orioles.

That same year, August "Gussie" Busch Jr. purchased the Cardinals. The grandson of brewing magnate Adolphus Busch, Gussie established the Anheuser-Busch Brewery as the world's largest and renamed Sportsman's Park Busch Stadium. The Cardinals, led by Bob Gibson and Lou Brock, won the World Series in 1964 and '67, and made it to the Fall Classic again in 1968.

A dominant Cardinals club emerged in the 1980s as Manager Whitey Herzog built a team around speed and defense to fit a new incarnation of Busch Stadium and its fast AstroTurf surface. Herzog led the Cards to the Series three

PLANES, TRAINS & AUTOMOBILES
Downtown St. Louis is a lively place on game days, but it's quieter at other times as the city is spread out over various neighborhoods. That, along with the oppressive summer heat and a minimal public transportation system, makes a car a must. Crank the air conditioning, go for a drive and enjoy the city's Midwestern hospitality.

A statue outside Busch Stadium honors hometown hero Stan Musial.

times and earned himself a ring in 1982. Tony La Russa took the reins as skipper before the 1996 season, and ushered in another winning era of Cardinals baseball, leading the team to a World Series title in 2006, the same season they moved into a new park, nicknamed Busch III. Their continued dominance in the NL is due in large part to All-Star first baseman, Albert Pujols, who is arguably the most feared hitter of his generation. In his first decade as a Redbird, "Prince Albert" consistently hit at least 30 homers and 100 RBI, bolstering a club ripe with talent. With fellow slugger Matt Holliday protecting him in the lineup and aces Adam Wainwright and Chris Carpenter at the top of a first-rate pitching staff to begin the new decade, the Cardinals have remained as competitive as ever.

THE RED SEA

Before it was fashionable to wear replica jerseys to games, Cards fans created a sea of red in the stands. Generations across several states grew up listening to KMOX broadcasters Harry Caray, Jack Buck and Bob Costas. The signal's reach helped the team build a vast regional following. Costas and Buck's son, Joe, have remained loyal St. Louis residents with ties to the Cardinals long after becoming national TV figures, known just as well for football and HBO programming as their baseball coverage.

The team reflects the loyalty St. Louis fans have to the city. Perhaps it's because the Cardinals, beginning in the 1920s, have appeared in the World Series in six different decades. It also helps that they have not endured three consecutive losing seasons since 1954–56, and have a classic logo that has remained with them since their inception. It certainly helps that one of the club's most legendary players, Stan Musial, is the type of down-to-earth gentleman that Midwesterners treasure. Not surprisingly, that tradition has followed through. What fans loved about "The Man" is what they cherish about Albert Pujols — who is fittingly known as "El Hombre."

Still, the unwavering attitudes of Cardinals fans come at a time when technology and the pace of life have made a lazy afternoon or evening at the ballpark seem outdated. St. Louis continues to embrace the team as fervently as it has for the last 110 years.

WHAT'S IN A NAME?

In 1899, St. Louis's new owner made a uniform change one of his first orders of business. Replacing the brown stockings — which had led to a previous moniker of the "Browns" — with bright red ones led *St. Louis Republic* sportswriter, William McHale, to creatively nickname the team Cardinals.

BUSCH LEAGUE

Although Sportsman's Park was located downtown, it never felt a part of the city because of its enclosed design. That was remedied in "new" Busch Stadium, which offers a grand view of the skyline, including the Gateway Arch.

The Gate 3 entrance on the west side of the stadium features a "bridge" resembling the city's famed Eads Bridge. That's also where a bronze statue of Stan Musial is located. Around the exterior of the stadium, marble plaques are embedded in the sidewalks, commemorating the Top 100 Cardinals Moments.

IN THE CARDS

The Cardinals Hall of Fame Museum is located in the International Bowling Hall of Fame and Museum building at 111 Stadium Plaza, between Clark and Walnut Streets. Grab a bite to eat at radio announcer and ex-Cardinal Mike Shannon's self-named restaurant. The steakhouse also serves as base camp for his local sports talk show after every home game. Ozzie's Restaurant and

Anheuser-Busch (far left) is prominent in St. Louis, and its trademark Clydesdales (center) are as common at the field as the Cards' mascot, Fredbird.

149

Sports Bar, named for Hall of Fame shortstop Ozzie Smith, is located on Washington Ave.

Big-time baseball card collecting shows still take place in St. Louis (where card trading originated), staged by St. Louis Sports Collectors and often featuring ex-Cards signing autographs.

LOOKING AT THE LOU

At 630 feet, the Gateway Arch is the nation's tallest man-made monument. A tram ride to the top is part of the riverfront experience, which can include the Museum of Westward Expansion, exhibits at the Historic Old Courthouse and sightseeing cruises.

Having been a fixture in St. Louis since 1853, Anheuser-Busch provides several tours of its vast operation. Visitors can see the Brew House, the Budweiser Clydesdale stable, lager cellar and packaging plant. The Beermaster Tour includes a trip to the finishing cellar and a sample directly from a tank.

St. Louis has more to offer than baseball and beer. The St. Louis Science Center offers more than 700 exhibits, a planetarium and an Omnimax theater. There's also the St. Louis Art Museum, built as the Fine Arts Palace of the 1904 World's Fair, and one of the nation's most comprehensive art museums.

If the summer heat isn't too intense, check out the Missouri Botanical Garden. The historic landmark offers 79 acres of landscaping and architecture. Or, you can go (free of charge) to the St. Louis Zoo in Forest Park. More than 800 species and 22,000 animals call the zoo their home.

Albert Pujols, who is worshipped by Redbirds fans, led the team to a World Series championship in 2006.

Kansas City

Widely known for its jazz, barbecue and vast baseball history, Kansas City retains an air of modest Midwest values, and the Royals are a product of that. K.C. boasts as varied a hardball history as any Big League city, but not surprisingly, the franchise has always had a knack for developing and keeping stars that fit the city's salt-of-the-earth personality.

PARIS OF THE PLAINS

Kansas City was home to arguably the most dominant Negro Leagues franchise and fielded teams in the Union Association, National League, American Association, Western Association and Western League, all before the start of the 20th century. One of eight founding American Association teams, the Kansas City Blues made their home in K.C. until 1954. The Blues served as an affiliate of the New York Yankees for their last 19 seasons and saw the rise of a young Mickey Mantle.

The American League's Athletics arrived from Philadelphia for the 1955 campaign and took up residence in Blues Stadium, which changed its name to Kansas City Municipal Stadium. Despite the leadership of Charles O. Finley, who bought the club in 1960 and the occasional presence of stars like Catfish Hunter on the roster, the club did not record a winning season in its 13 years in Kansas City before moving to Oakland. When the team departed after the 1967 season, Missouri Senator Stuart Symington threatened to introduce legislation that challenged baseball's antitrust exemption unless Kansas City received an expansion team. The AL awarded the city a franchise for the 1971 season, but Symington demanded the timetable be moved up to 1969.

After two successful years, the Royals left Municipal Stadium for the baseball-only Royals Stadium built by Owner Ewing Kauffman, which opened in 1973. From 1975–89, the Royals reached the playoffs seven times and won the 1985 World Series. That successful era of Royals baseball encompassed most of the career of Hall of Fame third baseman George Brett, who spent his entire 21-season career in Kansas City. The fiery Brett was a key player in the Royals' rivalry with the New York Yankees and drew fans out to the ballpark in droves as he chased the .400 mark in 1980. He retired in 1993 with 3,154 hits and a .305 career average.

Royals Stadium was renamed Ewing Kauffman Stadium shortly before the owner's death in 1993, and has long been considered one of the game's most beautiful ballparks. For decades the Royals were contenders in the AL, not enduring a last-place finish until 1996, after baseball expanded to six divisions. The proud club never

PLANES, TRAINS & AUTOMOBILES

Kauffman Stadium is situated right off I-70, and it's difficult to think of a modern ball-park more synonymous with driving and vast parking lots. For those traveling by car, getting around Kansas City is just as easy as finding a spot at the ballpark.

Picturesque Kansas City is known as the "Paris of the Plains."

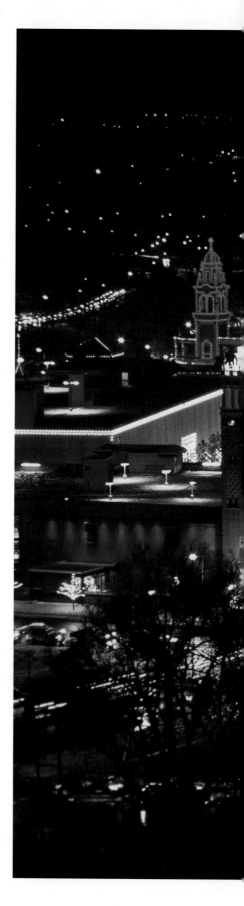

suffered a 100-loss season until 2002, its 34th season in the Big Leagues.

Ewing Kauffman, longtime owner of the Royals poured much of his pharmaceutical fortune into the team. Thanks to his dedication and the stellar play of lifetime Royals like Frank White and George Brett, the club ranked among AL attendance leaders for much of the 1970s despite a small facility and market.

Kauffman's death in 1993 and baseball's shifting economics have made things more challenging for the Royals, who no longer can rely solely on superior scouting and an occasional shrewd trade to win pennants.

Royals fans remain faithful to a team that reflects their city's traditional Midwestern values. Staying true to their identity, the team's classic uniforms have barely changed since the '70s, and Royals fans have seen a new star rise in the form of 2009 AL Cy Young Award winner Zack Greinke.

THE BIG KC
In 2003, ESPN.com ranked Kansas City's Kauffman Stadium as the Majors' sixth-best fan experience. And that was before a $250 million renovation was completed in 2009. Kauffman had aged gracefully before the facelift, but now it features modern amenities and design upgrades, including 360-degree concourses and a slew of kids' attractions including mini golf, a "Little K" diamond, batting tunnel and video arcade.

For a relatively small stadium in a city that takes pride in its small-town feel, the Royals haven't been shy about living large at Kauffman Stadium. The high-definition scoreboard added during the renovation is baseball's largest and stands 105-feet tall and 84-feet wide. Beyond the outfield fence is the park's signature feature: a 322-foot-wide water spectacular that ranks as the world's largest privately funded fountain.

In 2007, the Royals placed a red seat behind home plate amid a sea of blue to honor Negro Leagues legend Buck O'Neil. The seat was regularly occupied by O'Neil during his days with the club as a scout. Since the renovation, it can

be found in Section 127, Row C, Seat 9. It gets awarded each game to a community nominee who has distinguished him or herself with service to others.

No trip to Kansas City is complete without barbecue, and there are many options at Kauffman Stadium, including Rivals Sports Bar, located just beyond the fountain in right field.

FIT FOR A MONARCH
As the home of the Kansas City Monarchs, the longest running franchise in the Negro Leagues, Kansas City is the ideal location for the Negro Leagues Baseball Museum. The museum opened largely due to the efforts of the beloved Buck O'Neil, and showcases this important era of American history. Located adjacent to the American Jazz Museum in the 18th and Vine District, the museum offers interactive exhibits, the highlight being the "Field of Legends," which features life-size bronze figures of stars including Josh Gibson, Satchel Paige and Jackie Robinson.

Just a 20-minute drive north of the stadium is Chappell's Restaurant and Sports Museum, which holds the nation's largest collection of sports memorabilia on display in a restaurant.

THROUGH THE VINE
Kansas City isn't just barbecue and baseball, although one could be forgiven for focusing on those specialties.

The Liberty Memorial and the World War I Museum are must-sees for history buffs, and the top of the Liberty

Memorial provides a spectacular 360-degree view of the city.

With dozens of restaurants and more than 150 shops, Country Club Plaza was the nation's first outdoor shopping, dining and entertainment district, and might be Kansas City's most popular attraction. Another prime dining choice is Union Station, home to Science City, which offers planetarium shows and exhibits. The Nelson-Atkins Art Museum, known for stunning neo-classical architecture, houses one of the country's most impressive collections. Just east of Kansas City in Kingsville, Powell Gardens has more than 900 acres of botanical gardens that change with the seasons.

To unwind, the Kansas City Riverboat Casinos offer restaurants, theaters and shopping — a safe bet for a good time, even for those who avoid games of chance. Night owls will also like the 18th and Vine District, where they'll find restaurants and live jazz performances.

WHAT'S IN A NAME?
When the 1969 expansion put an AL franchise in Kansas City, the club held a naming contest. Looking for a title fit for a king, the winning entry was the Royals. Whether intentional or not, the name also pays tribute to the Kansas City Monarchs, longtime kings of the Negro Leagues.

George Brett (left) and the Negro Leagues' Monarchs ruled Kansas City.

BIBLIOGRAPHY

CHAPTER 1

22. "Magadan: There's a lot of dedication" Williams, Pete. "Where the (talented) boys are: three regions" *USA Today Baseball Weekly*. 11 March 1992. pg. 28-29.

CHAPTER 2

38. "Strong enough to cool 2,500 single-family homes" Williams, Pete. "The D'backs are asking fans: 'What about BOB?'" *USA Today Baseball Weekly*. 28 January 1998. pg. 8-9.

40. "The touring Philadelphia Phillies" Center, Bill. "Petco Park's opening is a homecoming for baseball in downtown San Diego" *San Diego Union-Tribune*. 4 April 2004.

CHAPTER 3

67. "The Mariners feature local vendors" Emmons, Natasha. "Local Flavor and fresh delivery highlights of Safeco Field menu" *Amusement Business*. 12 July 1999.

68. "George Tabeau organized a club" Moss, Irv. "Denver: A Baseball Town" *The Denver Post*. 14 October 2007.

71. "Built on 1.4 million square feet of land" Williams, Pete. "Coors Field is born" *USA Today Baseball Weekly*. 5 April 1995. pg. 29-30.

71. "Coors Field also produces some of the game's best pizza" Neel, Eric. "Coors gives the Rocky Mountains a high" Published at ESPN.com; retrieved February 10, 2010.

CHAPTER 4

76. "Instead of building another" "Five Facilities Opening in 2010: Target Field" *Street & Smith's Sports Business Journal*. 25 January 2010. pg. 16.

80. "Baseball never smells so good" Caple, Jim. "A great place for a tailgate." Published at ESPN.com; retrieved Feb. 3, 2010.

CHAPTER 5

114. "Restaurants such as Johnny Rockets." Fisher, Eric. "Yankees subscribe to 'more is best' theory." *Street & Smith's Sports Business Journal*. 19 April 2009. pg. 4.

121. "Hulk of red brick and steel" Muret, Don. "Philadelphia freedom from the Vet" *Street & Smith's Sports Business Journal*. 26 April 2004. pg. 17.

PHOTO CREDITS

INDEX